Two Essays on Entropy

Two Essays on Entropy

RUDOLF CARNAP

Edited with an Introduction by Abner Shimony

UNIVERSITY OF CALIFORNIA PRESS
BERKELEY LOS ANGELES LONDON

University of California Press
Berkeley and Los Angeles, California

University of California Press, Ltd.,
London, England

ISBN: 0-520-02715-9
Library of Congress Catalog Card Number: 73-94444

Copyright © 1977 by The Regents of the University of California

Contents

Introduction vii

    References xx

1. The aim of the investigations 1

Essay I: A Critical Examination of the Statistical Concept of Entropy in Classical Physics. 3

Summary 3
    A Brief Formulation of My Main Point Concerning the Statistical Concept of Entropy. 4
    2. A system of qualitative classification 9
    3. Disorder and entropy for a classification system 12
    4. Boltzmann's entropy concept 20
    5. Boltzmann's H-theorem 30
    6. The problem of the definition of entropy for other than statistical descriptions 33
    7. Gibbs's statistical method 45
    8. Gibbs's definition of entropy for an ensemble 50
    9. An alternative definition of entropy for an ensemble 58
    10. Entropy and amount of information 64

Essay II: The Abstract Concept of Entropy and its Use in Inductive Logic. 75

Summary 75
    11. The abstract entropy concept 77
    12. A simpler scheme without weights 85
    13. Degree of information 89
    14. Application to a scheme with one magnitude 95
    15. Regional systems 106

Introduction

CONCERNING THE TEXT

Carnap's two essays on entropy were written during his tenure of a fellowship at the Institute for Advanced Study in Princeton between 1952 and 1954. The Autobiography in the Library of Living Philosophers volume tells about conversations concerning entropy with mathematicians and physicists in Princeton.

> I certainly learned very much from these conversations; but for my problems in the logical and methodological analysis of physics, I gained less help than I had hoped for. At that time I was trying to construct an abstract mathematical concept of entropy, analogous to the customary physical concept of entropy. My main object was not the physical concept, but the use of the abstract concept for the purposes of inductive logic. Nevertheless, I also examined the nature of the physical concept of entropy in its classical statistical form, as developed by Boltzmann and Gibbs, and I arrived at certain objections against the customary definitions, not from a factual-experimental, but from a logical point of view. It seemed to me that the customary way in which the statistical concept of entropy is defined or interpreted makes it, perhaps against the intention of the physicists, a purely logical instead of physical concept; if so, it can no longer be, as it was intended to be, a counterpart to the classical macro-concept of entropy introduced by Clausius, which is obviously a physical and not a logical concept. The same objection holds in my opinion against the recent view that entropy may be regarded as identical with the negative amount of information. I had expected that in the conversations with the physicists on these problems, we would reach, if not an agreement, then at least a clear mutual understanding. In this, however, we did not succeed, in spite of our serious efforts, chiefly, it seemed, because of great differences in point of view and in language. [1963, pp. 36–37]

Because of the discouraging reception of his ideas, Carnap abandoned his original plan to publish the two essays together, and then decided against the immediate publication of the two separate essays. They are listed separately under "To Appear: New Works" in Carnap's Bibliography [Benson 1963, p. 1054], but according to Professor Arthur Benson he had kept open the possibility of making revisions.

The decision of Carnap's literary executors to publish the two essays together is reasonable, since it permits the reader to see his program in its entirety. The decision, however, necessitates some editorial changes in the typescript. The most important is the elimination of the first three sections of the second essay, for they were inserted only in order to make the second essay self-contained. This elimination requires the renumbering of the sections and formulas of the second essay. Since section 1, "The aim of the investigation," concerns both essays, it has been placed so as to serve as a preface to both. It was tempting, in fact, to go back entirely to the original scheme and simply call the two essays "Part I" and "Part II" respectively of a single work, which Carnap had named "An Abstract Concept of Entropy." The main reason for not doing so is that his original title is not at all descriptive of the contents of the first essay (or part), which in the editor's opinion is the more interesting of the two. One can conjecture that Carnap's original choice of title was indicative of his initial intentions, as indicated in the first paragraph of §1, but that in the course of working out his ideas he was drawn more deeply into the subsidiary problem than he had anticipated. The final important editorial change is the placement of "A Brief Formulation of My Main Point Concerning the Statistical Concept of Entropy" at the beginning of Essay I, without a section number. This placement accords fairly well with the following footnote to "A Brief Formulation...":

> I felt that a reader of the lengthy discussions in my article might be in danger of losing sight of my main point. Therefore I give here a brief formulation of this point, so that objections can be more easily focused on it. I intend to insert these formulations into §1 of the article.

The editor has corrected without notification a few obvious slips in the typescript.

CRITICAL EXAMINATION OF THE STATISTICAL CONCEPT OF ENTROPY

Any simple classification of conceptions of entropy is certain to be inadequate because of the many considerations involved: various levels of description, the large number of components in a thermodynamic system, permutability of identical components, dynamics of an isolated system, interaction of a system with different types of environment, uncertainty and information, and experimental control. One rough way of classifying conceptions, however, which is of great philosophical interest, is along a spectrum from entropy as an objective physical property to entropy as a nonphysical (perhaps subjective, perhaps logical or epistemological) concept. Of the two great classical masters of statistical mechanics, Boltzmann and Gibbs, the former was somewhat closer to the objective end of the spectrum and the latter to the nonphysical end, but in fact the conceptual differences between them were probably much less sharp than some of their respective followers have made out. Carnap unequivocally locates himself at the extreme physical end of the spectrum, and by giving a lucid formulation and defense of this conception of entropy he has made a significant contribution to the literature on the subject. Unfortunately, a full exposition of the other extreme of the spectrum did not exist at the time that Carnap wrote his essay, even though the nonphysical conception was "in the air." Had Jaynes's information-theoretical formulation of statistical mechanics [1957] been available to Carnap, his essay might have gained both in sharpness of focus and in historical accuracy, by taking the formulation of Jaynes rather than of Gibbs as the target in his analysis of the relation between entropy and uncertainty.

The core of Carnap's argument is given in §6. Entropy in thermodynamics is asserted to have the same general character as temperature, pressure, heat, etc., all of which serve "for the quantitative characterization of some objective property of a state of a physical system." The thermodynamic description of a system is presumably correct, but it is very coarse in comparison with the precise microscopic description D^{prec}, which in classical mechanics consists in the specification of the positions and momenta of all the constituent particles. In order to relate the thermodynamic description to finer descriptions, including the most precise one, the thermodynamic concepts must have counterparts defined in terms of the microscopic theory. For Carnap, a controlling principle in the search for such counterparts is *the principle of physical magnitudes*, essentially asserting that if a physical quantity is ascribed a definite value (with a certain precision) at a given time by a coarse description, then a finer description of the system at the same time must ascribe a compatible value to the quantity. To use the terminology which Carnap has recommended elsewhere [1950, p. 3], his principle is a partial *explication* of "physical quantity," and indeed a very plausible one. Both the constructive and the critical parts of Carnap's essay are almost corollaries of the foregoing statements.

Carnap's main constructive result (§5–§6) concerns a monatomic dilute gas in an insulating container, the diluteness guaranteeing that the energy of interaction per particle is negligible compared to the average kinetic energy of individual particles. His treatment is modeled upon that of Boltzmann, who supposed that the 6-dimensional μ-space ("μ" for "molecule," 3 dimensions for position, 3 for momentum) available to a particle was divided into a number K of cells, where K is much greater than 1 but much less than the number N of particles, so that the average number of particles per cell is not too small. A specification of the numbers N_j ($j = 1, \ldots, K$) of particles in each of the cells is called by Carnap "a statistical description," D^{st}. Boltzmann's own concept of entropy can be expressed in terms of the statistical description as

$$S_B(D^{st}) = -k \sum N_j \ln N_j + C,$$

where C is a constant depending on N but otherwise independent of the N_j, and the factor k (Boltzmann's constant) has only the significance of relating a combinatorial expression to standard physical units. Carnap then proposes an extension of Boltzmann's concept,

$$S_B^1(D_i) = S_B(D^{st})$$

for any description D_i which implies D^{st}, i.e., is consistent with D^{st} and at least as fine. The extended concept evidently satisfies the principle of physical magnitudes. What Carnap proposes is in the spirit of Boltzmann's objective and microphysical approach to the foundations of thermodynamics, and it is even more evidently in the spirit of the monograph of Boltzmann's disciples, P. and T. Ehrenfest [1959, especially sections 14c, 24c, and 28]. (Indeed, Carnap's essay can be profitably read together with this monograph, for he presents fully some ideas which are highly condensed by the Ehrenfests, while they present physical considerations, such as ergodicity, which are lacking in Carnap's exposition. Mutual illumination is especially provided by the Ehrenfests' sections 14c and 14d, and Carnap's discussion of the H-theorem in §9.)

Carnap restates Boltzmann's results on the agreement of statistical entropy S_B and thermodynamic entropy S^{th} as follows. Let Δt be a time interval of duration sufficient for the measurement of a macroscopic quantity like temperature or pressure, and let D_{typ}^{st} (not Carnap's notation) be a typical D^{st}, in the sense that its cell numbers equal approximately the respective averages of the time-varying cell numbers N_j during Δt. Boltzmann gave arguments which are powerful, though—because of difficulties in ergodic theory—not entirely definitive, that if the gas has been kept in isolation sufficiently long, then D_{typ}^{st} will with overwhelming probability be such as to make $S_B(D_{typ}^{st})$ very close to the maximum value of S_B compatible with the constraints of fixed energy, volume, and number of particles. (Lebowitz and Penrose [1973] present an excellent summary of the problems and results of ergodic theory.) He also showed that this maximum is equal to the value of Sth when the gas is in equilibrium under the given constraints. Carnap's general position suggests at this point an option, which he does not mention, of making thermodynamic as well as statistical entropy satisfy the principle of physical magnitudes by simply identifying S^{th} with $S_B(D^{st}_{typ})$. The agreement of statistical and thermodynamic entropy would thereby become a tautology, and Boltzmann's fundamental result would be restated, with no loss in depth, as asserting that S^{th} (interpreted as a time-averaged microscopic quantity) has with overwhelming probability the value predicted by thermodynamic theory and also the value obtained by standard operations for measuring entropy.

Another way (called "Method II" by Carnap) of extending Boltzmann's concept to descriptions other than D^{st} is to define the following concept:

$$S^{II}_B(D_i) =_{Df} k \ln m(D_i) + C'.$$

where D_i is equivalent to the disjunction of m individual descriptions (i.e., descriptions specifying the cell to which each of the N individual particles is assigned, rather than merely giving the occupation numbers of the cells). By proper choice of the constant C' the equality of $S^{II}_B(D^{st})$ and $S^I_B(D^{st})$ is easily established. Unlike $S^I_B(D_i)$, however, $S^{II}_B(D_i)$ does not satisfy the principle of physical magnitudes, as can be seen by considering a D^{st} which does not assign all particles to the same cell. Because of the permutability of the individual particles,

$$m(D^{st}) = \frac{N!}{N_1! N_2! \ldots N_k!},$$

which is in general greater than 1. But for any individual description D^{ind}, $m(D^{ind}) = 1$. Hence, even if D^{ind} implies D^{st} one has the inequality

$$S^{II}_B(D^{st}) \neq S^{II}_B(D^{ind}),$$

contrary to the principle of physical magnitudes. Since the entropy as defined by Method II depends upon the specificity of the description D_i, it is a logical or epistemological rather than a physical concept. Those statistical mechanicians who conceive of entropy as a measure of lack of information are committed to something like Method II.

Gibbs's innovations were motivated by an aim at generality (whereas Boltzmann's methods were most appropriate to systems with a large number of identical particles, preferably weakly interacting) and also freedom from dubious assumptions about the microscopic constitution of matter [1948, pp. ix–x]. Accordingly, he represents the state of a physical system with f degrees of freedom (where f is very large in the case of a thermodynamic system) not by occupation numbers in the cells of μ-space, but by a point U in a $2f$-dimensional phase space, with f dimensions for the generalized coordinates and f for the conjugate momenta. Incidentally, Carnap is incorrect in crediting Gibbs with introducing this representation into statistical mechanics, for Boltzmann had previously considered ensembles of systems described by a density $\rho(U)$ over the phase space [1871]. What Gibbs did that was entirely new was to identify thermodynamic quantities with parameters or functionals of $\rho(U)$. He examines a number of possibilities regarding entropy. [1948, ch. XIV, "Discussion of Thermodynamic Analogies"]; see also the commentary by Epstein [1936, pp. 491–509]. The concept which Carnap attributes to Gibbs is

$$S_G^{II}(D_i) = -k \sum_n P_i(Q_n^\gamma) \ln P_i(Q_n^\gamma) + \text{const.}$$

(8-3, 8-5, slightly rewritten). Here the phase space has been divided into cells Q_n^γ of finite volume, and $P_i(Q_n^\gamma)$ is the probability that an arbitrary member of the ensemble is in Q_n^γ if the ensemble is described by the density $\rho_i(U)$ associated with the description D_i, i.e.,

$$P_i(Q_n^\gamma) = \int_{Q_n^\gamma} \rho_i(U)\, dU$$

(8-1, rewritten). $S_G^{II}(D_i)$ is thus the concept of entropy which the Ehrenfests call "coarse-grained" [1959, p. 54], in contrast with the fine-grained entropy $-k \int \rho \ln \rho\, dU$, which is not helpful in considerations of irreversibility since it is constant in time. Gibbs himself did not write down a formula which can be regarded as a transcription of the above expression for $S_G^{II}(D_i)$. The ascription to him of the concept of coarse-grained entropy is not on this account erroneous, for it is surely implicit in the discussion of irreversibility in the famous ch. XII, where no formulas are written, and Tolman's Gibbsian exposition [1938, pp. 165 ff.] makes essential use of it. Nevertheless, the fact that in the discussion of thermodynamic analogies Gibbs prefers to use either the fine-grained entropy, or else special expressions appropriate for particular ensembles, may indicate a different philosophical viewpoint than the one attributed to him by Carnap, a point which will be discussed in comment 4 below.

Carnap's objection to $S_G^{II}(D_i)$ as a statistical counterpart of thermodynamic entropy is evident, if D_i is permitted to be a description of arbitrary specificity. The more specific D_i is, presumably the more concentrated in fewer cells. Consequently, $S_G^{II}(D_i)$

depends upon the specificity of D_i and does not conform to the principle of physical magnitudes. Indeed, as Carnap explains in the paragraph containing 8-6, $S_G^{II}(D_i)$ has the characteristics of a concept constructed in accordance with Method II.

A number of comments will now be stated about the cogency of Carnap's critique of classical statistical mechanics. Some of them can be made with confidence, either in favor of Carnap's position or against it. Some, however, raise difficult problems, concerning which only brief summaries of arguments and references to recent literature can be given.

1. There are many thermodynamic entropies, corresponding to different degrees of experimental discrimination and different choices of parameters (Grad, [1961] and [1967]; Jaynes [1965]; but see cautions in Tisza and Quay [1963, footnote 22]). For example, there will be an increase of entropy by mixing samples of O_{16} and O_{18} only if isotopes are experimentally distinguished. Jaynes therefore claims that "*Even at the purely phenomenological level, entropy is an anthropomorphic concept. For it is a property, not of the physical system, but of the particular experiment you or I choose to perform on it.*" [1965, p. 398]. Carnap's point of view can clearly accommodate a multiplicity of thermodynamic entropies, to each of which the principle of physical magnitudes would be applied when statistical counterparts are sought. That human considerations dictate the use of one or another of this family of concepts does not detract from the objective character of each member of the family. (See Grünbaum [1973, ch. 19], for a criticism of Jaynes's statement.)

2. An objection may be raised against applying the principle of physical magnitudes below the phenomenological level. Entropy, generically, is associated with disorder, but it may not be possible to choose in a nonarbitrary way a quantitative measure of the disorder of a system without reference to the level of description. Suppose, for example, that a system is composed of Kn identical particles and the D^{st} describes the system as having n particles in each of the K cells of the μ-space. The disorder, at this level of description, is usually considered to be the maximum possible. However, a particular precise description D^{prec} may exhibit a highly ordered structure—such as locating the particles exactly at lattice points, or clustering of particles in pairs—even though D^{prec} is compatible with the maximally disordered D^{st}. Even if D^{prec} does not manifestly exhibit an ordered structure, it may contain a hidden order which will become apparent as the system evolves in accordance with the laws of dynamics: for example, the particles uniformly distributed at

time 0 may become concentrated in one cell at a time t (as in the "reversibility paradox"). To be sure, Carnap's principle of physical magnitudes could be satisfied *pro forma* by defining statistical entropy at a chosen level and simply disregarding order at finer levels of description; Carnap has done exactly this in defining $S_B^1(D_i)$, the chosen level being that of the statistical description D^{st}. Such a strategy, however, is open to the charge of arbitrariness.

It might be suggested that the arbitrariness be resolved by finding out what is the deepest level of description relevant to the operational quantities involved in actual measurements of entropy, quantities like flow of heat into a calorimeter and length of a column of mercury in a thermometer. The appropriate level could hardly be that of D^{st}, since some precise descriptions compatible with D^{st} imply that sequences of collisions between particles of the system and those of the thermometer and calorimeter will occur which are extremely improbable from the standpoint of D^{st}, and which will yield anomalous values of the measured quantities. For the same reason the level of description could not be chosen to be one using cells in the 12-dimensional space of pairs of particles, or even cells in the $6n$-dimensional space of n-tuples of particles for any small n; the reason is the large number of encounters with other particles that any one particle makes during the time Δt needed for a measurement, the mean time between two successive encounters of a hydrogen molecule with other hydrogen molecules at normal pressure and temperature, for example, being approximately 6.6×10^{-11} sec. (Chapman and Cowling [1961, p. 92]). If one goes all the way to D^{prec} in choosing the level of description, there are overwhelming technical problems in computing the degree of order, and some conceptual problems as well.

3. The difficulty of formulating a nonarbitrary objective concept of the order of a system suggests that it may be simpler and more appropriate to define the microscopic counterpart of thermodynamic entropy in terms of randomness rather than of disorder. In ordinary discourse and in much of the literature of statistical mechanics the two words are used almost interchangeably. A clear and useful distinction is made between them, however, in an unpublished paper, "The Concept of Degree of Order," which is referred to in §2 of the present work:

> The term '*randomness*,' as defined in statistics, refers to a physical characteristic of the *procedure of selection* of a sample (class or sequence) from a given population. A procedure is defined to be random if all possible samples of the same size (or certain specified kinds of samples) have equal probability (in the statistical sense) to be selected.

Hence randomness is *not* a characteristic of the mathematical structure of a sample.... Any sample may be selected by a random procedure. (Therefore the term 'random sample' is misleading.) On the other hand, the degree of disorder is a characteristic of the mathematical structure.

Immediately following this distinction are remarks which are very suggestive for the problem of entropy:

The concepts of randomness and degree of disorder, although different, are inductively connected. If we know that a procedure of selection is random, we can determine the probability of the occurrence of certain kinds of samples and the expectation value of certain parameters with respect to samples. On the other hand, the inductive inference from the evidence describing a given sample S to the hypothesis h that S was produced by a random procedure is very weak and chiefly negative.... In no case can the mere inspection of a sample lead to the acceptance of h. This holds even if the sample is very large and, in addition, the values of the relevant parameters in the population are given.

Though Carnap's remarks are quite general, they surely allow the possibility of a randomizing procedure which is such that with overwhelming probability the degree of disorder at many levels of description is near the maximum. Knowledge of the randomizing procedure may also permit the calculation of the probabilities of nonnegligible discrepancies between the degree of disorder at one level and at another. By contrast, if one is told only that at the level of D^{st} the disorder is maximum, the probability that the state was produced by a random procedure may be low, as Carnap points out, or hard to determine, and therefore one cannot be confident about the degree of disorder at deeper levels of description. N particles may have been partitioned equally into K cells for the purpose of equitable distribution of booty, or for artistic simulation of randomization, or because the dynamics is such as to destroy correlations at that level but not (in the time allowed) at a deeper level; in all these cases one might expect high order at some deeper level than D^{st}. It follows that if entropy is defined in terms of the randomizing, it may provide more information about disorder at various levels than does an entropy concept defined in terms of the disorder at a chosen level. The mechanism of randomization, which may involve both dynamics and considerations of large numbers, can establish a reliable, though probabilistic, linkage among the interesting statistical features at various levels of description, whereas the principle of physical magnitudes establishes a rigid and nonprobabilistic link that may entirely miss the most interesting features at deep levels.

4. Gibbs's treatment of entropy can now be reconsidered with the foregoing remarks on random procedures in mind. Entropy, in

most of Gibbs's formulations is a functional of a density $\rho(U)$ on the phase space. Now suppose that $\rho(U)$ is established by some random physical procedure for selecting the state of the system, and is not merely a compendium of the observer's knowledge. Then an entropy defined in terms of ρ is directly related to randomness (although it is related indirectly and probabilistically to disorder, by the argument of the preceding paragraph). Now Gibbs's chapter XIV is most naturally read as suggesting that $\rho(U)$ is specified by a physical procedure—a suggestion that is lost, perhaps, in earlier chapters because of the abstractness of the treatment. (Note the remark by Klein [1970, p. 130] that ch. XIV is the climax of the development of Gibbs's ideas.) In particular the canonical distribution is appropriate for a system which has reached equilibrium with a heat reservoir, for contact with the reservoir is a mixing or randomizing procedure, the result of which is the selection of states according to the canonical distribution. Carnap's critique of Gibbs in §8 pays no attention to the physical circumstances relevant to Gibbs's own choices of $\rho(U)$. Instead, Carnap constructs a series of examples in which $\rho(U)$ is determined only by rather artificial knowledge of the observer. It is not surprising that the entropy calculated as a functional of such a distribution is unrelated to thermodynamic entropy.

5. In the reading of Gibbs suggested here, $\rho(U)$ may be understood to be a probability distribution in the "propensity" sense. The propensity interpretation of probability seems to have been formulated explicitly first by Peirce, who considered the probability that a tossed die will turn up a certain face to be "a certain 'would—be,' and to say that a die has a 'would-be' is to say that it has a property, quite analogous to any habit that a man might have" [1932, p. 409]. The name "propensity" is due to Popper, whose interest was mainly in the sense of probability appropriate to quantum mechanics [1957]. The probability distribution has an objective status in nature, according to the propensity interpretation, not, however, as the constitution of any actual ensemble, but rather as the weighted set of potentialities of outcomes in a type of physical situation. Both Peirce and Popper arrived at a propensity interpretation of probability after first espousing a frequency interpretation and then realizing that in most cases of interest the population or collective in which the relative frequencies are to be found does not actually exist. Since Gibbs considers the ensemble described by $\rho(U)$ to be virtual [1948, p. 17], it is much more natural to attribute to him a propensity than a relative frequency sense of probability.

Attractive as a propensity interpretation of probability may be, it is undoubtedly very obscure. Popper is inclined to take it as a primitive concept, but if one wishes to use the concept in the context of classical physics, where the fundamental laws are deterministic, then it appears to be illegitimate merely to postulate the existence of propensities without grounding them in dynamics. There is at least one way in which the concept of propensity can be explicated dynamically, namely via ergodic theory. (For an explanation of the terminology used here see Lebowitz and Penrose [1973]; and for a more extended discussion of the relation between propensity and ergodicity see Friedman and Shimony [197*]). Suppose that for a given physical system T an energy surface is metrically indecomposable. Then the microcanonical distribution is justified by the fact that for almost all trajectories on the surface the time spent by the phase point in any subset of the surface is asymptotically proportional to the measure of the subset. Suppose further that T is an isolated system consisting of a very large part R (reservoir) and a relatively small part σ, which interact with each other. Then for almost all trajectories on the energy surface of T, the time spent by σ in a subset of its phase space is proportional to the integral of an appropriate canonical distribution over that subset. In other words, the randomizing procedure of interaction with R almost certainly has the effect of making σ "visit" all states accessible to it with frequencies prescribed by the canonical distribution. The proof by Sinai of the metrical indecomposability of energy surfaces of a gas of hard spheres can be considered to legitimate the propensity interpretation in one very important class of cases. It is still a matter of research how far Sinai's result can be extended, and also whether properties weaker than metrical indecomposability will suffice to provide a dynamical justification for the distributions used in statistical mechanics (Grad [1967, pp. 69 ff.]; Khinchin [1949, chs. 5 and 6]).

6. A strong dissent to the foregoing reading of Gibbs is expressed by Jaynes, who considers him to be using probability in the epistemic sense of reasonable degree of belief [1967, p. 97]; note that Jaynes sometimes characterizes this sense of probability as "subjective," but always in quotation marks, and indeed many of his remarks in this paper and elsewhere indicate a commitment to something like a logical concept of probability. Whether or not Jaynes is historically accurate regarding Gibbs, it is important to assess his claim that the appropriate probability concept for statistical mechanics is epistemic probability, and that the concept of entropy is accordingly a measure of "amount of uncertainty" [ibid,

p. 97]. Carnap's exhibition of the discrepancy between S_G^{II} and S^{th} in cases 1 through 6 of §8 constitutes a serious objection to Jaynes's program. These cases are revealing, because in them the information upon which the computation of $\rho_i(U)$ is to be based is quite different from the usual kinds of information about the preparation of a system, e.g., that it is in contact with certain reservoirs. Consequently, in these cases it is easy to distinguish epistemic probability from probability in the sense of propensity, and it is difficult to borrow from the latter in evaluating the former. An entirely different objection to Jaynes's program is that his maximum-entropy prescription for evaluating probabilities can be saved from inconsistency with the calculus of probability only by a highly implausible assumption about prior probabilities (Friedman and Shimony [1971]). Finally, the incorrectness of conflating thermodynamic entropy with uncertainty in an information-theoretic sense can be illustrated by noting that in molecular biology the latter depends upon the number of isomers or well-defined variants of a type of molecule, a number which is independent of the thermodynamic entropy (Tisza and Quay [1963, VI]). Maintaining a clear conceptual distinction between thermodynamic entropy and information-theoretic uncertainty is, however, consistent with acknowledging that the price of acquiring information is always an increase of entropy, as Szilard discovered and Carnap lucidly explains in §10. A wonderful example is the increase of entropy due to the chemical reaction required for the "recognition" of an isomer (Monod [1971, p. 39]).

7. An exclusive commitment to taking statistical entropy to be a functional of $\rho(U)$ is by no means entailed by the above defense of Gibbs. Since an ensemble described by a canonical or microcanonical distribution will contain some (though relatively very few) members with anomalously high order at the level of D^{st} (or any other level of interest), it certainly is useful to have in one's arsenal of concepts a measure of disorder at this level, especially in treating the fluctuations that occur at thermodynamic equilibrium. The following passage is a judicious statement of the value of conceptual pluralism:

> The Boltzmann entropy of a particular system at a particular time t depends only on its observational state at that time; its statistical entropy, on the other hand, depends on what ensemble the system is to be regarded as belonging to, that is, on the experimental procedure to which the system was subjected before time t and which, if replicated many times, would generate this ensemble.... Thus the two definitions of entropy refer to different physical situations and are, in a sense, complementary. (Penrose [1970, p. 215])

It may be added that both Boltzmann's and Gibbs's concepts of entropy are physical and objective, though in different ways.

AN ABSTRACT CONCEPT OF ENTROPY

Although Carnap prefers an extended version of Boltzmann's concept of statistical entropy to that of Gibbs, he has some misgivings about Boltzmann's reliance upon a cell system in μ-space. The value of $S_B^1(D^{\text{prec}})$ depends on the size of the cells and the exact locations of their boundaries, both of which are arbitrary. Furthermore, as the system evolves in time, with D^{prec} changing continuously in accordance with the laws of motion, S_B^1 changes discontinuously as molecules pass from one cell to another. The main achievement of Carnap's second essay is the formulation of a concept of entropy S^{**} which is free from both of these defects. He also indicates how S^{**} could be applied in inductive logic.

The definition of S^{**} presupposes the concept of the *environment* of the point b_i occupied by the ith molecule, which is the set of all points in the μ-space closer to b_i than to any point occupied by another molecule. S^{**} is then defined (Eq. 11-10) in terms of the volumes of the environments of the system, and it is indeed independent of the choice of a cell system and continuous in its temporal evolution. Furthermore, S^{**} is a natural and aesthetically pleasing concept.

It may be questioned, however, whether S^{**} is free from arbitrariness. Some of the earlier objections concerning the order of a system at various levels of description can be readily modified so as to apply to S^{**}. Suppose, for example, that all of the N environments have equal volumes, so that S^{**}, and therefore the disorder which it measures, are maximized. The system would nevertheless be highly ordered, in an intuitive sense, if the equality of volumes of the environments were achieved by a perfectly regular lattice arrangement of the N molecules. Another source of arbitrariness is the expression "closer to" in the definition of "environment." If the point b_i in the μ-space is specified by a sextuple x_i^1, x_i^2, x_i^3, p_i^1, p_i^2, p_i^3 of position and momentum coordinates, then the distance between b_i and b_j depends not only upon the "position distance" $|\mathbf{x}_i - \mathbf{x}_j|$ and the "momentum distance" $|\mathbf{p}_i - \mathbf{p}_j|$, for both of which there are natural metrics, but it also depends upon the relative weights placed upon these two "distances"; but neither kinematics nor dynamics supplies a nonarbitrary method of assigning relative weights. By contrast, the dynamical theorem of Liouville does provide a natural volume measure in the phase space of the N

molecules, from which follows a natural volume measure in the μ-space of a single molecule; and in Boltzmann's procedure, using a cell-system, the volume measure suffices to compute the entropy.

It is hard to assess the potential value of S^{**} in inductive logic, especially since Carnap himself did not seem to make much use of it in his work on induction between 1954 and 1970 (cf. Carnap and Jeffrey [1971]). Possibly the difficulty in computing S^{**}, which has a geometrical character in contrast to the combinatorial concept S_B, discouraged him from applying it. The complications in §14 and §15, which treat relatively simple cases, show that a strong motivation would be needed to justify the effort of calculating S^{**} in practical situations.

Apart from the relative merits of S^{**} and S_B, Carnap's second essay is interesting as a continuation of his pioneering work on the relations among the concepts of confirmation, order, and entropy ([1952] and Carnap and Bar-Hillel [1952]). Recent developments of this active line of investigation in inductive logic are reported in two collections edited by Hintikka and Suppes, [1966] and [1970].

Acknowledgements: The editor is grateful to Professor Arthur J. Benson and to Professor Charles R. Willis for their very helpful suggestions and their encouragement. The research was supported in part by the National Science Foundation.

References

BAR-HILLEL, Y., and CARNAP, R.
    [1952] "Semantic Information," *British Journal for the Philosophy of Science*, 4, 147–157.

BENSON, Arthur J.
    [1963] "Bibliography of the Writings of Rudolf Carnap," in *The Philosophy of Rudolf Carnap* (Library of Living Philosophers, Vol. XI). Ed. P. A. Schilpp. La Salle, Ill.: Open Court.

BOLTZMANN, Ludwig
    [1871] "Zusammenhang zwischen den Sätzen über das Verhalten mehratomiger Gasmoleküle mit Jacobi's Princip des letzten Multiplicators," *Wiener Berichte* 63, 397. (Reprinted in *Wissenschaftliche Abhandlungen*, ed. Fr. Hasenöhrl, vol. 1 [Leipzig, 1909].)

CARNAP, Rudolf
    [1950] *Logical Foundations of Probability*. Chicago: University of Chicago Press.

[1952] *The Continuum of Inductive Methods.* Chicago: University of Chicago Press.
[1963] "Intellectual Autobiography," in *The Philosophy of Rudolf Carnap*, ed. P. A. Schilpp. La. Salle, Ill.: Open Court.
[Unpublished] "The Concept of Degree of Order."

CARNAP, R., and JEFFREY, R.
[1971] *Studies in Inductive Logic and Probability.* Vol. I. Berkeley, Los Angeles, London: University of California Press.

CHAPMAN, S., and COWLING, T. G.
[1961] *The Mathematical Theory of Non-Uniform Gases.* Cambridge: Cambridge University Press.

EHRENFEST, P., and EHRENFEST, T.
[1959] *The Conceptual Foundations of the Statistical Approach in Mechanics.* Ithaca: Cornell University Press. Translated by M. J. Moravcsik from *Encyclopädie der mathematischen Wissenschaften.* Vol. IV 2 ii. Leipzig: Teubner, 1912.

EPSTEIN, Paul S.
[1936] "Critical Appreciation of Gibbs' Statistical Mechanics," in *A Commentary on the Scientific Writings of J. Willard Gibbs.* Vol. II. Ed. A. Haas. New Haven: Yale University Press.

FRIEDMAN, K., and SHIMONY, A.
[1971] "Jaynes's Maximum Entropy Prescription and Probability Theory," *Journal of Statistical Physics*, 3, 381-384.
[197*] "The Propensity Interpretation of Probability."

GIBBS, J. Willard
[1948] *Elementary Principles in Statistical Mechanics*, in *Collected Works of J. Willard Gibbs.* Vol. II. New Haven: Yale University Press. Reprinted from edition of 1902.

GRAD, Harold
[1961] "The Many Faces of Entropy," *Communications on Pure and Applied Mathematics*, 14, 323-354.
[1967] "Levels of Description in Thermodynamics and Statistical Mechanics," in *Delaware Seminar in the Foundations of Physics.* Ed. M. Bunge. New York: Springer.

GRÜNBAUM, Adolf
[1973] *Philosophical Problems of Space and Time.* 2nd ed. Dordrecht: Reidel.

HINTIKKA, J., and SUPPES, P.
[1966] *Aspects of Inductive Logic.* Amsterdam: North-Holland.
[1970] *Information and Inference.* Dordrecht: Reidel.

JAYNES, E. T.
[1957] "Information Theory and Statistical Mechanics," *Physical Review*, 106, 620-630 and 108, 171-190.
[1965] "Gibbs vs. Boltzmann Entropies," *American Journal of Physics*, 33, 391-398.
[1967] "Foundations of Probability Theory and Statistical Mechanics,"

in *Delaware Seminar in the Foundations of Physics*. Ed. M. Bunge. New York: Springer.

KHINCHIN, A. I.
   [1949] *Mathematical Foundations of Statistical Mechanics*. New York: Dover. Translated from the Russian by G. Gamow.

KLEIN, Martin
   [1970] *Paul Ehrenfest*. Vol. I. Amsterdam: North-Holland.

LEBOWITZ, J., and PENROSE, O.
   [1973] "Modern Ergodic Theory," *Physics Today*, 26 no. 2, 23–29.

MONOD, Jacques
   [1971] *Chance and Necessity*. New York: Knopf. Translated from the French by A. Wainhouse.

PEIRCE, Charles S.
   [1932] *Collected Papers*. Vol. II. Ed. C. Hartshorne and P. Weiss. Cambridge, Mass.: Harvard University Press.

PENROSE, Oliver
   [1969] *Foundations of Statistical Mechanics*. Oxford: Pergamon.

POPPER, Karl R.
   [1957] "The Propensity Interpretation of the Calculus of Probability, and the Quantum Theory," in *Observation and Interpretation*. Ed. S. Körner. London: Butterworths.

TISZA, L., and QUAY, P.
   [1963] "The Statistical Thermodynamics of Equilibrium," *Annals of Physics*, 25, 48–90. Reprinted in L. Tisza. *Generalized Thermodynamics*. Cambridge: M.I.T. Press, 1966.

TOLMAN, Richard
   [1938] *The principles of Statistical Mechanics*. Oxford: Oxford University Press.

1. The Aim of the Investigations

Summary. This section indicates briefly the purpose of this work. The aim is the construction of an abstract concept of entropy, which is to serve as a basis for a definition of degree of confirmation for a quantitative language. This construction (in Essay II) is preceded (in Essay I) by a critical analysis of the statistical concepts of entropy in classical physics (Boltzmann, Gibbs). The abstract concept is intended to apply to a system of N elements, each characterized by the values of n magnitudes ϕ_i with continuous scales. Each element is represented by a phase point in the n-dimensional phase space (μ-space).

The chief aim of this work is the construction of an abstract (i.e., purely mathematical) concept of entropy which is to fulfill the following three purposes:

(1) It is intended to measure the *disorder* exhibited by a system of N elements, where each element is characterized by the values of n magnitudes; the concept is to be a continuous function of these values.

(2) The concept is to serve as a basis for defining *inductive probability* ("degree of confirmation") for systems of the kind mentioned. This will constitute the first step in the extension of inductive logic, which has so far been developed only for qualitative descriptions,[1] to universes described in quantitative terms.

(3) The concept is to supply, as a special case, a modified version of *the entropy concept in classical physics*; since the concept is a continuous function, it avoids the arbitrary system of cells used in Boltzmann's definition.

The definitions of the abstract concept of entropy and of a concept of degree of confirmation based on it will be given in Essay II, together with theorems of inductive logic based on these definitions. This will be preceded by a discussion in Essay I of the nature of the statistical concept of entropy in classical physics. This analysis will provide valuable heuristic clues for the construction of the definition of the abstract concept. But, independently of this aim, the discussion will also point out what seem to be serious disadvantages in the customary extended version of Boltzmann's definition and in Gibbs' definition of entropy and to suggest alternative definitions. In close connection with this critical analysis, an attempt

---

[1] R. Carnap, *Logical Foundations of Probability* (Chicago: University of Chicago Press, 1950); hereafter referred to by '(Prob.)'.

will be made to clarify the controversial problem of the relation between entropy and amount of information.

I shall now briefly indicate the general features of a system to which the abstract concept of entropy is intended to apply. The system consists of N elements a_i ($i = 1, \ldots, N$; $N \geq 2$) and n functions ϕ_j ($j = 1, \ldots, n$; $n \geq 1$). Each function has for each element a real number as its value: $\phi_j(a_i) = u_{ij}$. The system is supposed to be completely described by the nN numbers u_{ij}.

As an example, the elements may be the molecules of a body of gas g at a given time t. This physical system is *identified* by its location (say, in a given container in our laboratory) and time t; it is *described* by a statement of the values of n magnitudes for each of the N molecules; in the simplest case, we have $n = 6$ magnitudes, viz. the three position coordinates and the three momentum components. A description of this kind will be called a *precise description* (D^{prec}) of the system, in distinction to other, less specific descriptions (§4).

We assume that for each ϕ_j a set of *admitted values* is given. Unless otherwise indicated, this set is assumed to be an interval of the ϕ_j-scale. (In the example of the gas, the position coordinates are bounded by the vessel containing the gas, the velocity by the velocity of light.)

Each element a_i is represented by its phase point b_i in the n-dimensional phase space, called the μ-*space* (module space); the coordinates of b_i are the values $u_{i1}, \ldots, u_{in}$. Thus the system is represented by the N phase points $b_1, \ldots, b_N$. It is assumed that a set of *admitted phase points* is specified, called the *total range* R^μ; it is a subset of (in the simplest case, identical with) the set of those points in the μ-space whose coordinates are the admitted values of the functions ϕ_j. We assume that a Lebesgue measure function is defined for certain subsets of the phase space, such that the measure or "volume" of an n-dimensional subset defined by one interval for each function ϕ_j is the product of the lengths of these n intervals. Thus the volume V^μ of R^μ is less than or equal to the product of the lengths of the n intervals of admitted values. Hence V^μ is always finite.

Essay I: A Critical Examination of the Statistical Concept of Entropy in Classical Physics

Summary. The first sections (§§2–3) contain preliminary discussions. For a simple classification system, the following concepts are defined: degree of order o^* and degree of confirmation c^* (§2); degree of disorder d^* and entropy S^* (§3). The main body of Essay I deals with the concept of entropy in classical statistical mechanics and its relation to the thermodynamic concept of entropy (S_{th}). First, Boltzmann's definition of entropy (S_B, §4) and his H-theorem (§5) are explained. S_B applies only to statistical descriptions (D^{st}). Two methods for extending it to other forms of descriptions, especially individual descriptions (D^{ind}), are discussed (§6). It is shown that the customary extended concept S_B^{II} is not generally in agreement with S_{th} and is a logical rather than a physical concept. An alternative extended concept S_B^I is proposed, which is a physical concept and is generally in agreement with S_{th}. Gibbs's method of representing a description of a state of a gas by an ensemble in the γ-space is explained (§7). Gibbs's entropy concept S_G^{II} is examined (§8); it is similar to S_B^{II} and has the same disadvantages. It is shown that Gibbs's theorem to the effect that S_G^{II} increases in the course of time is not an analogue to the second law of thermodynamics. An alternative S_G^I for Gibbs's S_G^{II} is defined which avoids the disadvantages of the latter (§9). A theorem on S_G^I is formulated which is an analogue of the second law. Some authors equate entropy with negative amount of information. For D^{st}, the two values are indeed equal. However, the relation holds for other descriptions only if S_B^{II}, not S_B^I, is chosen, hence only if the physical character and the agreement with S_{th} are sacrificed (§10).

A Brief Formulation of My Main Point Concerning the Statistical Concept of Entropy

A. GENERAL REMARKS ON MACRO- AND MICRO-MAGNITUDES.

Let W be a physical macro-magnitude (e.g., volume or mass of a body), for which a measuring procedure is established which, according to experience, yields in any given case (of the kind to which W is applicable) a definite value of W independently of subjective factors of the observer (e.g., his preferences or prior information). Then we may say that W is an *objective* concept. (I shall later, in §6, use the more specific term 'purely physical magnitude' and give more exact criteria for it.) For the question of the objectivity of a magnitude W it makes no difference whether the value of W is directly measured or indirectly determined, i.e., calculated according to established rules from directly measured values of other magnitudes. If the latter magnitudes are objective physical concepts, then W is likewise.

According to a basic assumption of classical physics (usually not formulated explicitly) the result of a measurement of W for a physical system s at a given time t_1 depends upon the micro-state of s at t_1. Let us formulate this assumption more exactly. The process of measurement does actually extend over a certain period of time around t_1, say Δ_1, and covers a certain spatial region R containing s. The assumption means that, for any objective physical macro-magnitude W there is a *corresponding micro-magnitude M*, i.e., one which fulfills the following conditions:

(1) There are some of the *fundamental micro-magnitudes* (e.g., electro-magnetic field, gravitational field, electric charge, mass, position of particles, etc.) which are relevant for W, say $M_1, \ldots M_j, \ldots$.

(2) The value of M for any region R and any period Δ can be defined as a function of the distribution of the magnitudes M_j within R during Δ.

(3) If W is applicable to the state of s during Δ_1, then $W(s, \Delta_1) = M(R, \Delta_1)$. (This agreement between M and W is either meant to hold exactly or to be such that the value of W lies with high probability within a small interval around the value of M.)

Since the fundamental micro-magnitudes of classical physics were conceived as objective, M is likewise objective. (The relativity of a physical magnitude with respect to a basis of reference, e.g., zero point, unit, scale form, coordinate system or the like must not be misunderstood as subjectivity.) This means that the value of M is dependent only on the objective micro-situation, not on the information possessed by the observer X. (Needless to say, X's knowledge of M, that is, his estimate of the actual value of M, depends upon his information concerning observational results.)

Let D_0 be the complete description of the distribution of the values of the magnitudes M_j within R during Δ_1. Let D_0, $D_1, \ldots D_n, \ldots$ be a series of descriptions of R during Δ_1, such that D_{n+1} is weaker than D_n (i.e., D_{n+1} is deducible from D_n but not vice versa) and such that each description D_n of the series is sufficient for the determination of M for R and Δ_1. Let the value of M derived from D_n be $M(D_n)$. Obviously the values $M(D_0)$, $M(D_1), \ldots$ must all be equal, because all these descriptions, being deducible from the true complete description D_0, are likewise true and hence cannot lead to a value of M different from the actual value of M for R and Δ_1 as given by $M(D_0)$.

B. APPLICATION TO ENTROPY.

We shall now apply the above considerations to thermodynamic entropy (S_{th}), a macro-magnitude of classical thermodynamics. For simplicity, we consider the state of an isolated gas body g during the time period Δ_1 around t_1. Let the vessel containing the gas be divided into two chambers separated by a wall. To assure the applicability of S_{th}, we assume that the gas is during Δ_1 in a state of local thermodynamic equilibrium (§5); this means that the temperature is the same throughout each chamber and throughout Δ_1, and the same holds for the pressure. Temperature and pressure are directly measurable macro-magnitudes. The entropy S_{th} is not immediately measurable. Its value for g at t_1 (relative to some final state of g, say, the state of total equilibrium with temperature and pressure equalized throughout the vessel) can be determined by a series of measurements during a slow (quasi-reversible) transition process leading from the given state to the chosen final state. On the other hand, S_{th} for g at t_1 can also be calculated with the help of the laws of thermodynamics from the following data: the kind of gas (say, hydrogen), and for each chamber its volume and the values of temperature and pressure of the gas in the chamber at t_1. Thus S_{th} can be determined on the basis of measurable, objective macro-magnitudes; hence S_{th} is itself an objective macro-magnitude.

The micro-theory for thermal processes in gases is the kinetic theory of gases which applies the methods of statistical mechanics to the molecules of the gas. Thus the problem arises of defining in terms of this theory statistical micro-magnitudes corresponding to the thermodynamic macro-magnitudes, in particular, to S_{th}. It is found that the fundamental micro-magnitudes relevant for the thermodynamic macro-magnitudes are the following: the mass of a molecule (which is the same for all molecules of a given substance), and for each molecule at a given time certain state-coordinates (in the simplest case, that of a sufficiently diluted monatomic gas, there are six of these, viz., the three position coordinates and the three momentum components). Thus the task is to define on this basis a suitable statistical concept of entropy.

Solutions of this problem were proposed by Boltzmann and Gibbs. *Boltzmann* applied his concept S_B only to descriptions of a certain kind (I shall call them statistical descriptions, D^{st}) which are much weaker than complete micro-descriptions D_0. Later physicists proposed a generalization of S_B, which I shall denote by 'S_B^{II}'; this concept is applicable to descriptions of various series D_0, D_1, D_2, etc., as described above. We find that the resulting values of S_B are not exactly equal for any two of the descriptions, and show for some of them even enormous differences, one value being a large multiple of the other. Since all these descriptions are true micro-descriptions of the same gas g for the same period Δ_1 around t_1, at most one of the resulting values of S_B^{II} can exactly agree with the value of S_{th} for g at t_1 as determined from measurements made during Δ_1, and some will diverge widely from S_{th}.

The statistical entropy concept proposed by *Gibbs*, which I shall denote by 'S_G^{II}', has the advantage of being applicable to a much wider class of cases than Boltzmann's concept and to a greater variety of logical forms of descriptions. But S_G^{II} shares with Boltzmann's concept the feature just explained; its value varies in the given series of descriptions. Therefore S_G^{II} cannot possibly agree generally with S_{th}. *This is my main objection* against both S_B^{II} and S_G^{II}. It seems the generally accepted view among physicists that S_B^{II} and S_G^{II} are adequate micro-magnitudes corresponding to S_{th}. I believe that the facts stated refute this view.

The variation of both concepts in the above-mentioned series of descriptions shows also that both concepts are not objective. Today many physicists seem to recognize this. I shall show, moreover, that either concept is purely logical; that is to say, a statement which ascribes to g during Δ_1 *a specific value of either S_B^{II} or S_G^{II} does not give any information at all concerning the physical state of g. This is my second main objection* to the view that these concepts correspond to S_{th}. The result just stated follows from the fact that the value of either magnitude calculated on the basis of a micro-description, depends merely upon the strength or *amount* of information of the description, not on its *content*; in other words, the value is determined merely by *how much* the description says, not by *what* it says.

Some physicists today believe that the non-objective (or not purely objective) character is inevitable for any statistical concept of entropy. (Incidentally, some believe the same even for a statistical concept of temperature.) This view is in conflict with the principle, implicitly accepted by physicists in the classical period, that for any objective macro-magnitude there must be a corresponding objective micro-magnitude. In defense of this principle I shall propose an alternative S_B^I to Boltzmann's S_B^{II} and an alternative S_G^I to Gibbs's S_G^{II} such that the following conditions are fulfilled if S is either S_B^I or S_G^I:

(1) S is an objective physical micro-magnitude; that is, a statement of a specific value of S for g during Δ_1 gives some information about the physical state of g.

(2) The value of S is the same for all descriptions of the series D_0, D_1, etc.

(3) The value of S determined on the basis of any of these descriptions is in agreement with the value of S_{th} for g during Δ_1. (The definition of S_B^I is constructed in a very simple way. Since it is known that for any D^{st}, S_B^{II} is in agreement with S_{th}, I define S_B^I in such a way that it has for any D^{st} the same value as S_B^{II}, and then I assign to it for any other description of the same series this same value. Thus the three conditions are fulfilled. The guiding idea for the definition of S_G^I is analogous but somewhat more complicated.)

2
A System of Qualitative Classification

Summary. In a classification of K cells Q_j ($j = 1, \ldots, K$), an individual description (D^{ind}) assigns each of the N elements to one cell. A statistical description (D^{st}) states merely the number N_j of elements of each cell Q_j. Z is the number of all D^{ind}; z is the number of those D^{ind} which correspond to a given D^{st}. The degree of order o^* of a D^{ind} is defined as $1/z$. A measure function m^* for the D^{ind} is defined, which is proportional to o^*. With its help, the degree of confirmation c^* is defined.

As a preliminary to the study of systems with quantitative magnitudes, we shall consider in this and the next section the much simpler case of classification systems. Here the N elements are characterized by qualitative properties Q_j ($j = 1, \ldots, K$) which form a classification or division (i.e., each element has one and only one of the K properties). The K properties Q_j are also called the *cells* of the classification. A complete description of the system specifies for each element the cell to which it belongs. A description of this kind is called an *individual description* D^{ind}.

(2-1) The number of individual descriptions for given N and K is $Z = K^N$.

Throughout this section, 'D' without superscript (with or without subscript) refers to a D^{ind}. For a given D_i, let N_j ($j = 1, 2, \ldots, K$) be the number of elements belonging to the cell Q_j. The numbers $N_1, \ldots, N_K$ are called the *cell numbers* in D_i. D_1 and D_2 are said to be *statistically equivalent* if they have the same cell numbers.

A description of the system of N elements which states for each cell Q_j merely its cell number N_j (but does not say *which* elements belong to Q_j) is called a *statistical description* D^{st}.

(2-2) (a) The number of D^{ind} with the cell numbers $N_1, \ldots, N_K$ is

$$z = \frac{N!}{N_1! \ldots N_K!}.$$

In other words:

(2-2) (b) Let D_i^{ind} be an individual description with the cell numbers $N_1, \ldots, N_K$ and D_i^{st} be the corresponding statistical description. Let $z(D_i^{ind})$ be the number of D^{ind} statistically equivalent to

D_i^{ind}, and $z(D_i^{st})$ the number of D^{ind} corresponding to D_i^{st}; then

$$z(D_i^{ind}) = z(D_i^{st}) = \frac{N!}{N_1! \ldots N_K!}.$$

(2-3) z has its *minimum* in the case that all elements belong to the same cell ("homogeneous system"), hence one cell number is N and all others 0:

$$z_{min} = 1.$$

(2-4) z has its *maximum* in the case that all cell numbers are as nearly equal as possible (i.e., the difference between any two is 0 or 1). Let us assume, for simplicity, that N is divisible by K; then

$$z_{max} = \frac{N!}{\left(\frac{N}{K}\right)!^K}.$$

The traditional concept of regularity or uniformity is often used in philosophical discussions, e.g., in the postulate of the uniformity of the world as an allegedly necessary presupposition of induction. This concept is meant in such a sense that one system (possible world) is regarded as more regular than another if more or stronger laws (either universal or statistical) hold in the one than in the other. Let us try to explicate this concept, at least for certain cases, in a quantitative form as "degree of order" of a D^{ind}, denoted by '$o(D^{ind})$'. At another place (not yet published) I have analyzed in greater detail the traditional concept mentioned and the conditions which an adequate explicatum o must fulfill. I have shown that with respect to simple classification systems, the function o must fulfill the following requirements:

(2-5) *First requirement.* For given N and K, $o(D)$ depends only on the cell numbers; in other words, if D_1 and D_2 are statistically equivalent, $o(D_1) = o(D_2)$.

(2-6) *Second requirement.* $o(D)$ is a symmetric function of the cell numbers in D.

(2-7) *Third requirement.* Let D_2 be formed from D_1 by shifting an element from one cell to another cell which had in D_1 the same or a higher cell number than the first cell. Then

$$o(D_2) > o(D_1).$$

It is easily seen that, among others, the following function o^* fulfills the requirements mentioned:

(2-8) $$o^*(D) =_{Df} \frac{N_1! \ldots N_K!}{N!} = \frac{1}{z(D)}.$$

Once a suitable function o is found, it seems plausible (as I have explained at the other place) to define on its basis the *degree of confirmation* in the following way. The degree of confirmation $c(h, e)$ of a hypothesis h with respect to the evidence e is definable in terms of a measure function m (expressing the initial inductive probability or the degree of confirmation on the null evidence) as follows ((Prob.) §55A):

(2-9) $$c(h, o) =_{Df} \frac{m(e. h)}{m(e)}.$$

Now it seems plausible to choose the function m in such a way that $m(D)$ is proportional to $o(D)$. The factor of proportionality is uniquely determined by the condition that the sum of m for all D^{ind} must be 1. Then we take, in the usual way, $m(h)$ for any statement h as the sum of m for those D^{ind} in which h holds ((Prob.) §55A). Applying this procedure to the function o^* defined by (2-8), we obtain the following function m^*:

(2-10) $$m^*(D) =_{Df} \frac{N_1! \ldots N_K!(K-1)!}{(N+K-1)!}.$$

Then we define:

(2-11) $$c^*(h, e) =_{Df} \frac{m^*(e. h)}{m^*(e)}.$$

The same functions m^* and c^*, derived in a different way without the use of degree of order, were suggested by me (first in 1945) as a basis of a system of inductive logic ((Prob.) §10).

Let e be a D^{ind} for the elements $a_1, \ldots, a_n$, and n_j the cell number of Q_j in e. Let h_j be the hypothesis that another element a_{n+1} belongs to Q_j. The following result is easily derived from (2-10) and (2-11):

(2-12) $$c^*(h_j, e) = \frac{n_j + 1}{n + K}.$$

3
Disorder and Entropy for a Classification System

Summary. The degree of disorder d^* is defined as $1/o^* = z$. In analogy to Boltzmann's definition, we define the entropy S for a classification system as a linear function of the logarithm of $d^*(=z)$. We choose a particular function S^* of this form, defined as $\text{Log}(a/z)$ ('Log' denotes the logarithm to base 2).

For the further discussions in Part I, we shall leave aside the problems of inductive logic, to which we shall return in Part II. Our main topic in Part I will be the problem of entropy. The aim of the present section is to define disorder and entropy for classification systems. If any function o is chosen as degree of order, let us take as *degree of disorder d* its reciprocal:

(3-1) $$d(D) =_{\text{Df}} \frac{1}{o(D)}.$$

We apply this to o^* (2-8) and define:

(3-2) (a) $\quad d^*(D) =_{\text{Df}} \dfrac{N!}{N_1! \ldots N_K!}$

(b) $\quad\quad\quad = z(D).$

Since a given D_i^{st} is characterized by the set of cell numbers which holds for each of the corresponding D^{ind}, and since d^* depends merely on these cell numbers, it seems natural to ascribe that value of d^* which those D^{ind} have in common to D_i^{st} also. Therefore we define:

(3-3) (a) $\quad d^*(D_i^{\text{st}}) =_{\text{Df}} \dfrac{N!}{N_1! \ldots N_K!}$

(b) $\quad\quad\quad = z(D_i^{\text{st}}).$

Hence:

(3-4) If D_i^{st} corresponds to D_i^{ind},
$$d^*(D_i^{\text{st}}) = d^*(D_i^{\text{ind}}).$$

From (2-3):

(3-5) $$d^*_{\min} = 1.$$

From (2-4):

(3-6) $$d^*_{max} = \frac{N!}{\left(\frac{N}{K}\right)!^K}.$$

In order to obtain for a classification system a concept S of *entropy* analogous to Boltzmann's concept (§4), we shall define S as a linear function of the logarithm of the degree of disorder d^*, which is equal to z. (We write 'ln' for the natural logarithm.) Since Boltzmann defined his concept only for D^{st}, we shall at present do the same. Later, however, we shall apply our concept also to D^{ind}.

Thus for given N and K and for a given D_i^{st}, $S(D_i^{st})$ is obtained by multiplying $\ln z(D_i^{st})$ by a constant coefficient (>0) and adding another constant. The two constants may depend upon N and K. Therefore we shall represent them as functions $f(N, K)$ and $g(N, K)$, respectively:

(3-7) $S(D_i^{st})$ shall have the form $f(N, K) \ln z(D_i^{st}) + g(N, K)$ with suitably chosen functions f and g.

We wish the entropy to be a monotone increasing function of disorder; therefore

(3-8) For any N and K, $f(N, K) > 0$.

With the help of Stirling's theorem, we have the following *approximation*, where $r_j = N_j/N$:

(3-9) (a) $$\ln z = \ln \frac{N!}{\prod_j N_j!} \cong N \sum_j \left(r_j \ln \frac{1}{r_j} \right)$$
$$+ \frac{1}{2}\left(\ln N - \sum_j \ln N_j \right) - (K-1) \ln \sqrt{2\pi},$$

(b) $$\cong N \sum_j \left(r_j \ln \frac{1}{r_j} \right).$$

We lay down the convention that the value of $u \ln u$ (and hence also of $u \ln 1/u$) for $u = 0$ is to be taken as 0 (since this is the limit of the function for $u \to 0$). The cruder approximation (3-9)(b) is applicable only if N is very large; its use is customary in statistical mechanics. From (2-3):

(3-10) $$\ln z_{min} = 0.$$

From (2-4) with (3-9):

(3-11) (a) $\ln z_{max} \cong \left(N + \dfrac{K}{2}\right) \ln K - \dfrac{K-1}{2} \ln N - (K-1) \ln \sqrt{2\pi},$

(b) $\cong N \ln K$, if N is very large in relation to K.

Applying (3-9)(b) to (3-7):

(3-12) For large N, $S(D_i^{st})$ shall have approximately the form

$$F(D_i^{st}) = F(N, K, N_1, \ldots, N_K) = N \sum_j \left(r_j \ln \dfrac{1}{r_j}\right) f(N, K) + g(N, K).$$

We are free to choose the functions f and g in (3-7). We shall now lay down two requirements which seem desirable for our purposes, and then we shall choose as f and g two functions f_2 and g_2, respectively, such that these requirements are fulfilled for the form F in (3-12). Both requirements can be fulfilled for the form (3-7) only as approximations for large N; but the functions f_2 and g_2 thus determined will later be used in the definition of S generally, for any N.

(3-13) *First requirement.* If N varies but the relative frequencies r_j remain unchanged, F is to be proportional to N.

This means the following. Let D be a D^{st} characterized by N, K, and the values N_j. Let D' be analogous to D but with N', K', and N_j' such that $N' = mN$ with a fixed positive integer m, $K' = K$, and for every j, $N_j' = mN_j$, hence $r_j' = N_j'/N' = r_j$. Then, the requirement says that $F(D') = mF(D)$. Hence from (3-12) (with '$\sum(\ldots)$' for '$\sum_j \left(r_j \ln \dfrac{1}{r_j}\right)$'):

$mN \sum(\ldots) f(mN, K) + g(mN, K) = mN \sum(\ldots) f(N, K) + mg(N, K).$

$mN \sum(\ldots)[f(mN, K) - f(N, K)] = mg(N, K) - g(mN, K).$

If, for given N, K and m, the values N_j vary, $\sum$ varies but everything else remains constant. Therefore the factor of $\sum$ must be 0, and hence also the right side. Thus, for any N, K, m, $f(mN, K) = f(N, K)$ and $g(mN, K) = mg(N, K)$. Therefore:

(3-14) $f(N, K)$ is independent of N; we write '$f_1(K)$'.

The condition for g just mentioned is fulfilled if we put

(3-15) $\qquad g_1(N, K) =_{Df} N \cdot h(K),$

with an arbitrary function h. Hence:

(3-16) $\qquad F(\ldots) = N \sum (\ldots) f_1(K) + N h(K).$

(3-17) *Second requirement.* If each cell is subdivided into a fixed number p of new cells with equal cell numbers N_j/p, F is to remain unchanged.

Here we consider two D^{st}, D and D', with the following relations. The number of elements is the same in both: $N' = N$. Each cell in D corresponds to p cells in D' with equal cell numbers: $N_j = N'_{j1} + N'_{j2} + \ldots + N'_{jp}$; $N'_{j1} = N'_{j2} = \ldots = N'_{jp} = N_j/p$. Hence $r'_{j1} = \ldots = r'_{jp} = r_j/p$. Corresponding to each term in $\sum$ in (3-16) for D, there are for D' p equal terms $\frac{r_j}{p} \ln \frac{p}{r_j}$; their sum is $r_j \left(\ln \frac{1}{r_j} + \ln p \right)$. Thus we have, since $\sum r_j = 1$:

(3-18) $\qquad F(D') = N \left[\sum \left(r_j \ln \frac{1}{r_j} \right) + \ln p \right] f_1(pK) + N h(pK).$

According to (3-17), the right sides in (3-16) and (3-18) must be equal; hence:

$$\sum (\ldots) [f_1(pK) - f_1(K)] + \ln (p) \cdot f_1(pK) + h(pK) - h(K) = 0.$$

As in the earlier case, the factor of $\sum$ must be 0; hence $f_1(pK) = f_1(K)$. Thus f_1 must be a positive constant (see (3-8)), which we denote by 'A':

(3-19) $\qquad f_2(N, K) =_{Df} A \; (> 0).$

Then

$$A \ln (p) + h(pK) - h(K) = 0.$$

We put $h'(K) =_{Df} e^{h(K)} > 0$. Hence $h(K) = \ln h'(K)$. Therefore

$$\ln h'(pK) = \ln h'(K) - A \ln p = \ln [h'(K) p^{-A}].$$

Hence $h'(pK) = h'(K) p^{-A}$. Let $h'(K)$ have the form $\sum_n (C_n K^{E_n})$, where the exponents E_n and the corresponding coefficients C_n may be any real numbers. Then:

$$\sum (C_n p^{E_n} K^{E_n}) = \sum (C_n p^{-A} K^{E_n}).$$

Since this must hold for any K, coefficients of equal powers of K must be equal:

For any n, $C_n p^{E_n} = C_n p^{-A}$.

For any n, this condition is fulfilled if and only if either $C_n = 0$ or $p^{E_n} = p^{-A}$ and hence, for $p > 1$, $E_n = -A$. Therefore, for $E_n \neq -A$, all coefficients $C_n = 0$; for $E_n = -A$, C_n is arbitrary. Hence $h'(K) =_{\text{Df}} CK^{-A}$, with arbitrary C. Since $h'(K) > 0$, $C > 0$. We put $B = \ln C$. Then $h(K) =_{\text{Df}} B - A \ln K$; and from (3-15),

(3-20) $\qquad g_2(N, K) =_{\text{Df}} N(B - A \ln K).$

Thus our result is as follows:

(3-21) If $F(D_i^{\text{st}})$ is defined in the form

$$N\left\{A\left[\sum \left(r_j \ln \frac{1}{r_j}\right) - \ln K\right] + B\right\}$$

with arbitrary numerical constants $A(>0)$ and B, then F fulfills the requirements (3-13) and (3-17).

A function S of the form (3-7) has for large N approximately the form F (3-12). Therefore we decide to use in (3-7) those functions f_2 and g_2 which have been found to fulfill the requirements:

(3-22) $S(D_i^{\text{st}})$ shall have the form

$$A[\ln z(D_i^{\text{st}}) - N \ln K] + BN,$$

with constants $A(>0)$ and B to be chosen.

Any function S of this form fulfills the two requirements if N is large. The definition of S will not, of course, be restricted to large N; but the requirements cannot be fulfilled for all N by any function of the form (3-7); this can be seen by applying the requirements to the form (3-9)(a) instead of (3-9)(b).

If we had only to do with classifications, as in this section, the second requirement would not appear as essential, and therefore a simpler definition of S without the term '$-N \ln K$' would presumably appear as preferable. However, we introduce the concept of entropy for a classification chiefly as a model to guide our later construction of the abstract entropy concept. This concept will involve quantitative magnitudes, and therefore the invariance with respect to a subdivision of the cell system will be important.

We shall now define the function S^* as a special case of the form (3-22). We choose $B = 0$. Further, we shall use the logarithm to the base 2 (denoted by 'Log') because we intend to use S^*, together with d^*, o^*, m^*, and c^*, in inductive logic and in the theory of information, where the base 2 is convenient and customary. This makes it convenient to choose $A = 1/\ln 2$. Thus we define:

(3-23) $$S^*(D_i^{st}) =_{Df} \text{Log } z(D_i^{st}) - N \text{ Log } K.$$

(3-24) S^* fulfills the two requirements (3-13) and (3-17) approximately for large N.

With (2-1):

(3-25) $$S^*(D_i^{st}) = \text{Log } \frac{z(D_i^{st})}{Z}.$$

$z(D_i^{st})$ is the proportion of those D^{ind} which correspond to the given D_i^{st}; hence it is $< Z$. Therefore:

(3-26) For any D^{st}, $S^* < 0$.

According to (3-3), the relation between S^* and d^* is as follows:

(3-27) $$S^*(D_i^{st}) = \text{Log } d^*(D_i^{st}) - N \text{ Log } K.$$

With (3-9):

(3-28) (a) $$S^*(D_i^{st}) \cong N\left[\sum_j \left(r_j \text{ Log } \frac{1}{r_j}\right) - \text{Log } K\right]$$
$$+ \frac{1}{2}\left(\text{Log } N - \sum_j \text{Log } N_j\right) - (K-1) \text{ Log } \sqrt{2\pi},$$

(b) $$\cong N\left[\sum_j \left(r_j \text{ Log } \frac{1}{r_j}\right) - \text{Log } K\right], \text{ for large } N.$$

With (3-10) and (3-11):

(3-29) $$S^*_{min} = -N \text{ Log } K.$$

(3-30) (a) $$S^*_{max} \cong -\left[\frac{K-1}{2} \text{Log } N - \frac{K}{2} \text{Log } K + (K-1) \text{Log } \sqrt{2\pi}\right]$$

(b) $$\cong -\frac{K-1}{2} \text{Log } N, \text{ for very large } N.$$

We have defined S^* only for D^{st}. Now we introduce an extended concept S^{*I} which applies also to other descriptions, including D^{ind}. [The symbol 'S^{*I}' is chosen because the definition applies Method I to be explained later (§6); for an alternative extension S^{*II} see (10-15).] Let D_i^{ind} be any D^{ind} corresponding to D_i^{st}. Then, according to (2-2)(b), D_i^{ind} has the same value of z as D_i^{st}. Since now $S^*(D_i^{st})$ depends only on z and Z, we shall take as value of $S^{*I}(D_i^{ind})$ the value of $S^*(D_i^{st})$. We shall do the same for any other D^{ind} with the same z, even if it does not correspond to D_i^{st}, and also for any disjunction of D^{ind} with the same z. Thus we define S^{*I} as follows:

(3-31) If D_i is either a D^{ind} whose z is z_i or a disjunction of two or more D^{ind} for each of which z has the same value z_i, then

$$S^{*I}(D_i) =_{Df} \text{Log } \frac{z_i}{Z}.$$

Hence:

(3-32) For any D_i^{st}, $S^{*I}(D_i^{st}) = S^*(D_i^{st})$.

(3-33) If D_i^{ind} corresponds to D_i^{st}, $S^{*I}(D_i^{ind}) = S^{*I}(D_i^{st}) = S^*(D_i^{st})$.

Numerical example. For the sake of simplicity, we take an example with very few cells and round cell numbers. We consider *four statistical descriptions* for the same elements ($N = 10^6$) but with different cell systems. We consider first a D^{st} D_{16} with $K = 16$ cells. Since N is large, we may use (3-28)(b). Let $N_1 = 99,000$, hence $r_1 = 0.099$; $N_2 = 102,000$, hence $r_2 = 0.102$, etc.; the 16 values r_j (not the N_j) are stated in the subsequent table. The example is chosen in such a way that the first eight cell numbers are close to each other and considerably higher than the last eight, which are also close to each other. The values of $r_j \text{ Log } \frac{1}{r_j}$ are conveniently taken from Dolansky's table.[1]

---

[1] L. and M. P. Dolansky, Table of $\log_2 \frac{1}{p}$, $p \log_2 \frac{1}{p}$, etc. Res. Lab. of Electronics, M.I.T., Techn. Report No. 227, 1952.

EXAMINATION OF THE STATISTICAL CONCEPT OF ENTROPY 19

From the description D_{16} we derive another description D_8 with 8 cells by merging the first and second cells in D_{16} into a new cell, likewise the third and fourth cells, and so on; thus each r_j-value in D_8 is the sum of two r_j-values in D_{16}. By the same procedure D_4 with $K = 4$ is formed from D_8 and D_2 with $K = 2$ from D_4.

We see from the table that S^* has nearly the same value for all four descriptions. Each cell in D_2 is divided into two cells of D_4 with nearly equal cell numbers. If the cell numbers were equal, the values of S^* would be equal, because S^* fulfills the second requirement (for large N). Since there is a slight difference between the two cell numbers in each case, a small amount of order is introduced and hence S^* is slightly diminished. The same holds for the transition from D_4 to D_8, and finally to D_{16}.

The table lists furthermore the minimum and maximum values of S^* for each of the four given values of K, according to (3-29) and (3-30)(a), respectively.

γ (for D_{16})	r_j	D_{16} ($K=16$)		D_8 ($K=8$)		D_4 ($K=4$)		D_2 ($K=2$)	
		r_j	$r_j \text{Log} \frac{1}{r_j}$	r_j	$r_j \text{Log} \frac{1}{r_j}$	r_j	$r_j \text{Log} \frac{1}{r_j}$	r_j	$r_j \text{Log} \frac{1}{r_j}$
1	0.099		0.3303	0.201	0.4653	0.399	0.5289	0.800	0.2575
2	0.102		0.3359						
3	0.100		0.3322	0.198	0.4626				
4	0.098		0.3284						
5	0.103		0.3378	0.203	0.4670	0.401	0.5286		
6	0.100		0.3322						
7	0.101		0.3341	0.198	0.4626				
8	0.097		0.3265						
9	0.023		0.1252	0.045	0.2013	0.098	0.3284	0.200	0.4644
10	0.022		0.1211						
11	0.028		0.1444	0.053	0.2246				
12	0.025		0.1330						
13	0.026		0.1369	0.050	0.2161	0.102	0.3359		
14	0.024		0.1330						
15	0.025		0.1291	0.052	0.2218				
16	0.027		0.1407						
$\sum r_j \text{Log} \frac{1}{r_j}$		3.7208		2.7213		1.7218		0.7219	
Log K		4.		3.		2.		1.	
$\sum(\ldots) - \text{Log } K$		-0.2792		-0.2787		-0.2782		-0.2781	
$S^*(D)$		$-2.792 \cdot 10^5$		$-2.787 \cdot 10^5$		$-2.782 \cdot 10^5$		$-2.781 \cdot 10^5$	
$S^*_{\min}$		$-4 \cdot 10^6$		$-3 \cdot 10^6$		$-2 \cdot 10^6$		-10^6	
$S^*_{\max}$		-137.38		-67.04		-29.88		-10.29	

4
Boltzmann's Entropy Concept

Summary. Boltzmann's concept refers to the state of a gas g at time t consisting of N molecules. The μ-space is divided into cells Q_j of equal volume v^μ. A precise description (D^{prec}) gives the Nn values. The D^{ind} and D^{st} are as before. A macro-description (D^{mac}) states the results of measurements of temperature and pressure in the various parts of g. Boltzmann's definitions of a function H of the cell numbers N_j (4-3) and of entropy (S_B, (4-6)) are given. Both concepts apply to D^{st}. Boltzmann regards all D^{ind} as equally probable (4-8). Then for any D^{st}, S_B is a linear function of the logarithm of its probability (4-10). Boltzmann's definition has certain disadvantages; S_B is dependent upon an arbitrary cell system and is not a continuous function of the values of the magnitudes involved. The abstract concept to be defined later (in Part II) avoids these disadvantages.

Boltzmann[1] considers the state of gas body g at a given time t. g consists of N molecules, each characterized by n magnitudes ϕ_i. This is a special case of the kind explained in §1; but Boltzmann transforms it by the introduction of a cell system into a classification system (as discussed in §§2 and 3). For each magnitude ϕ_i, its interval of admitted values is divided into small intervals of equal length Δ_i. Hereby the μ-space is divided into a system Ω^μ of *cells* of equal volume $v^\mu = \Delta_1 \ldots \Delta_n$. Let K be the number of these cells within the total range R^μ; then:

$$(4\text{-}1) \qquad v^\mu = \frac{V^\mu}{K}.$$

These μ-cells Q_j ($j = 1, \ldots, K$) are analogous to the cells Q_j in the classification system (§3).

On the basis of a given cell system, Boltzmann makes a distinction, although not clearly and explicitly, which is essentially that between statistical descriptions D^{st} and individual descriptions D^{ind} as explained in §3. He speaks on the one hand of "eventualities" (op. cit. p. 40) or "state distributions" (p. 44), on the other hand of "equipossible cases". It is clear that he means by the former terms D^{st} or states described by D^{st} (called by other authors 'macroscopic states', 'macro-states', 'conditions' or simply 'states') and by the latter term D^{ind} or states described by D^{ind} (called by other authors 'microscopic states', 'micro-states', 'complexions' or

---

[1] L. Boltzmann, *Vorlesungen über Gastheorie*, Teil I (Leipzig: J. A. Barth, 1896).

simply 'states'). This interpretation of Boltzmann's distinction is apparent from the way he explains it by the analogy to drawings from an urn; he shows that here the number of "equipossible cases" "corresponding to an eventuality" with numbers $N_1, \ldots, N_K$ is $N!/(N_1! \ldots N_K!)$ (p. 39), which is our $z(D_i^{st})$. For greater clarity, we shall distinguish four kinds of descriptions for g at t.

First, a *precise description* D^{prec} states the nN values of the n magnitudes for the N molecules of g at t. An *individual description* D^{ind} of g at t with respect to Ω^μ specifies for each molecule a_i the cell in which its phase point b_i is located, in other words, it specifies for each a_i and each φ_j the interval of the φ_j-scale to which the value $\varphi_j(a_i)$ belongs. A *statistical description* D^{st} for g at t with respect to Ω^μ states the cell numbers.

Finally, let us divide the space occupied by (or at least available to) the gas in the vessel (not the phase space) into regions of equal volume ("macro-cells") just large enough to make it possible to measure in each region the momentary value of temperature and pressure, according to the technological knowledge available at the time in question. A *macro-description* D^{mac} states the results of these measurements.

The logical relations between the four kinds of descriptions are obviously as follows. Once a cell system Ω^μ has been chosen, a given D^{prec}, say D_i^{prec}, determines uniquely a certain D_i^{ind} based upon Ω^μ such that D_i^{prec} logically implies D_i^{ind}. D_i^{ind} does not imply D_i^{prec}; it contains less information. The same relation holds between D_i^{ind} and a certain D_i^{st}.

The relation between a D^{mac} and a D^{st} is more complicated. The measurement of a magnitude like temperature T or pressure p is not, strictly speaking, carried out at one time point but during a certain time interval Δt. If the cell numbers N_j were to remain constant during this interval, so that the same D^{st} would hold throughout, then the values of T and p can be determined from this D^{st} with the help of the laws of the kinetic theory of gases. If the cell numbers change during the interval, the same relations hold between the values of T and p on the one hand and the mean values $\bar{N}_j$ ($j = 1, \ldots, K$) where $\bar{N}_j$ is the mean of the number of molecules in Q_j during the interval. Let us say that D_i^{st} is *typical* for the interval Δt if the cell numbers stated in D_i^{st} are the mean cell numbers for the interval. If a typical D_i^{st} for an interval Δt is given and a suitable system of macro-cells is chosen, the corresponding D_i^{mac} can be determined (see §5). Inversely, D_i^{mac} determines, with respect to Ω^μ, the class C_i^{st} of the corresponding D_i^{st}, that is, those which, taken as typical for Δt, are compatible with D_i^{mac}. The results of measurements stated by D_i^{mac} are, strictly speaking, not point values but intervals. Therefore the class C_i^{st} contains a very large number of D^{st}. Thus it is a great oversimplification to say, as is often done, that a D^{st} is an appropriate representation of the observed state of a gas.

D_i^{st}, in turn, determines the class C_i^{ind} of the corresponding D^{ind}. D_i^{st} is logically equivalent to the disjunction of these D^{ind}. The same relation holds between D_i^{ind} and the corresponding class C_i^{prec}. (Thus the descriptions may be arranged in trees; see the diagram (10–19) below.) However, while C_i^{st} and C_i^{ind} are finite, C_i^{prec} would be infinite if we meant the D^{prec} to have absolute precision. Although the conception of classical physics, on which our discussions are based, regards it as meaningful to refer not only to finite intervals but also to point values of magnitudes and hence to an absolutely precise "state" as a system of such values, it is impossible to describe in a given language such values or states and it is all the more impossible, not only practically but even theoretically, to know such values or states. Therefore, strictly speaking, we ought to think of a D^{prec} not as something that could actually be given, but rather as an ideal which cannot actually be obtained but can be approached with any precision desired. Any such approximation to a D^{prec} is then really a D^{ind} with the size of the cells determined by the precision obtained.

The introduction of the system of cells is a very ingenious device by which Boltzmann transforms the problem of defining entropy within the framework of the kinetic theory into a problem concerning the simple schema of a K-fold classification. While in the kinetic theory (in its classical form) the possible states constitute an infinite and even nondenumerable set, in the K-schema the number of D^{st} and even that of D^{ind} is finite.

Let f_j be the density in Q_j, i.e., the number of molecules per unit of μ-volume:

$$(4\text{-}2) \qquad f_j =_{Df} \frac{N_j}{v^\mu}.$$

Boltzmann defines his H-function for a given D_i^{st} with cell numbers N_j as follows ('$\sum$' is short for '$\sum_{j=1}^{K}$'):

$$(4\text{-}3) \qquad H(D_i^{st}) =_{Df} \sum [f_j \ln f_j] v^\mu.$$

EXAMINATION OF THE STATISTICAL CONCEPT OF ENTROPY 23

Hence

(4-4). (a) $H(D_i^{st}) = \sum [N_j \ln N_j] - N \ln v^{\mu}$,

(b) $= -N\left\{\sum\left[r_j \ln \frac{1}{r_j}\right] - \ln N + \ln v^{\mu}\right\}$.

With the approximation (3-9)(b) for large N, (4-1), and (2-1):

(4-5) (a) $H(D_i^{st}) \cong -\ln z(D_i^{st}) + N[\ln N - \ln V^{\mu} + \ln K]$.

(b) $\cong -\ln \frac{z(D_i^{st})}{Z} + N \ln \frac{N}{V^{\mu}}$.

Boltzmann defines his statistical concept of entropy, which we denote by 'S_B', as follows:

(4-6) $\qquad S_B(D_i^{st}) =_{Df} -k H(D_i^{st})$,

where $k = 1.38 \times 10^{-16}$ erg/°C (the so-called Boltzmann constant). Hence:

(4-7) $\qquad S_B(D_i^{st}) \cong k\left\langle \ln \frac{z(D_i^{st})}{Z} + N \ln \frac{V^{\mu}}{N}\right\rangle$.

The purpose of Boltzmann's definition of S_B was to construct on the basis of the kinetic theory a concept corresponding to the *thermodynamic concept of entropy*, S_{th}, which had been introduced by Clausius. It was a stroke of genius for Boltzmann to discover that this purpose could be fulfilled by using a function of the form of his H. What remained was merely to adjust the constant in (4-6) in such a way that the new concept S_B would quantitatively agree with the old concept S_{th}. The latter could be defined in classical physics only relatively, i.e., only the difference of the entropies of two states of a physical system was defined, not their absolute values. Consequently, an arbitrary constant (i.e., a function dependent at most on N, K, and v^{μ}, but not on the N_j) may be added in (4-3) or (4-4). [This is often done in such a way that H is defined simply by $-N\sum\left(r_j \ln \frac{1}{r_j}\right)$. However, it is to be noted that in this case the additivity (4-11) does not hold.]

The numbers N_j characterize the state of the gas at one time moment; they vary greatly with time, even in very small intervals of time. Therefore H and S_B vary likewise (though at a much lower rate because H is, aside from an additive constant, the weighted mean of $\ln N_j$ over the cells with the N_j as weights, see [4-4](a)).

Since S_{th} is defined in terms of measurable magnitudes, it can at best agree with a mean of S_B for a time interval Δt (see the above remarks on D^{mac}). We shall come back to this point in the next section.

Boltzmann introduces a probability distribution (denoted here by 'pr_B') suggested by the experimental results, though not uniquely determined by them. (The term 'probability' is here to be understood in the statistical, not the inductive or logical sense.[2]) He first regards the probability that the phase point of any given molecule belongs to a given sub-region of the range R^μ as proportional to the volume of the sub-region. Therefore the probability that the phase point belongs to a given cell is $1/K$. Secondly, he takes the probabilities for different molecules as independent of each other. Therefore the Z D^{ind} have equal probabilities:

(4-8)   For every D_i^{ind}, $pr_B = \dfrac{1}{Z}$.

A D^{st} is a disjunction of the z corresponding D^{ind}; therefore:

(4-9) $$pr_B(D_i^{st}) = \frac{z(D_i^{st})}{Z}.$$

Hence with (4-7):

(4-10) $$S_B(D_i^{st}) \simeq k\left[\ln pr_B(D_i^{st}) + N \ln \frac{V^\mu}{N}\right].$$

Thus $S_B(D_i^{st})$ is a linear function of the logarithm of the probability of D_i^{st}. Boltzmann emphasizes this close connection between entropy and probability (pp. 38 ff); he shows that the second law of thermodynamics (see below, §5) is derivable as a probability statement (pp. 42, 60).

(4-11)   *Additivity of H and S_B.* If the gas g at t consists of p spatial parts g_m $(m = 1, \ldots, p)$, then, with respect to D^{st} for g and for its parts,

(a) $H(g) = \displaystyle\sum_{m=1}^{p} H(g_m)$,

(b) $S_B(g) = \displaystyle\sum_{m=1}^{p} S_B(g_m)$.

---

[2] Concerning this distinction, see (Prob.), §12.

EXAMINATION OF THE STATISTICAL CONCEPT OF ENTROPY

Proof. The parts g_m correspond to non-overlapping regions R_m of cells in the μ-space. Let $N^{(m)}$ be the number of molecules in g_m; $\sum_m N^{(m)} = N$. Then from (4-4)(a):

$$H(g_m) = \sum_{Q_i \text{ in } R_m} [N_i \ln N_i] - N^{(m)} \ln v^\mu.$$

Hence $\sum_m H(g_m) = \sum_{Q_i \text{ in } R^\mu} [N_i \ln N_i] - N \ln v^\mu = H(g)$. This is (a). (b) follows from (a) with (4-6).

We have, as is customary, assumed that the cells Q_i in the μ-space have equal volumes v^μ. This is essential for the derivation of (4-4), (4-5), (4-9), and (4-10). It may be remarked that for a definition of the form (4-3) this assumption is not necessary. We could use cells Q_j with different volumes v_j and define H by $\sum (f_j \ln f_j) v_j$. Suppose that two cells Q'_j and Q''_j with equal densities $f' = f''$ are merged into one new cell Q_j with $v_j = v'_j + v''_j$ (v'_j and v''_j need not be equal) and $N_j = N'_j + N''_j$. Then in Q_j, $f = f' = f''$. The two terms $(f' \ln f')v'_j$ and $(f'' \ln f'')v''_j$ in the $\sum$ for the first system are replaced for the second system by one term $(f \ln f)v_j$, which is equal to the sum of the two terms. Thus $\sum$ remains unchanged. These considerations will be of importance for our construction of an abstract concept of entropy (in Part II). There we shall make use of a system of cells (called "environments") of different volumes.

In the present schema, with equal cell sizes v^μ, we can make a fusion or a subdivision only if we do it for all cells simultaneously. A consideration like the one above leads to the following result.

(4-12) *Invariance of H and S_B with respect to a subdivision of calls.* Let D be a D^{st} for N molecules, based on a system Ω^μ of K cells Q_j ($j = 1, \ldots, K$) of volume v^μ with cell numbers N_j. Let D' be a D^{st} based on the system $\Omega^{\mu'}$ of pK cells of volume v^μ/p; each previous cell Q_j is here subdivided into p cells with equal cell numbers $N_{j1} = N_{j2} = \ldots = N_{jp} = N_j/p$. Then

   (a) $H(D) = H(D')$
   (b) $S_B(D) = S_B(D')$.

Proof. In D', for every i ($= 1, \ldots, p$), $r_{ji} = N_{ji}/N = N_j/pN = r_j p$. In (4-4)(b), the term $r_j \ln \dfrac{1}{r_j}$ in $\sum$ for D is therefore replaced in $\sum'$ for D'

by p equal terms $(r_j/p) \ln (p/r_j)$; their sum is $r_j[\ln (1/r_j) + \ln p]$. Thus, since $\sum r_j = 1$, $\sum' = \sum + \ln p$. $\ln v^\mu$ is replaced by $\ln (v^\mu/p) = \ln c^\mu - \ln p$. Therefore $H(D') = H(D)$.

The following theorems state maxima and minima for given N and V^μ (or N, K, and v^μ).

(4-13) For a uniform distribution (every $N_j = N/K$, every $r_j = 1/K$):

(a) $\sum \left(r_j \ln \dfrac{1}{r_j} \right)$ has its maximum $\ln K$.

(b) H has its minimum $-N \ln \dfrac{Kv^\mu}{N} = -N \ln \dfrac{V^\mu}{N}$ (from (4-1)).

(c) S_B has its maximum $kN \ln \dfrac{V^\mu}{N}$.

(4-14) For the case of all molecules concentrated in one cell (one $N_j = N$, one $r_j = 1$, all others 0):

(a) $\sum \left(r_j \ln \dfrac{1}{r_j} \right)$ has its minimum 0.

(b) H has its maximum $N(\ln N - \ln v^\mu) = N \ln \dfrac{NK}{V^\mu}$.

(c) S_B has its minimum $-kN(\ln N - \ln v^\mu) = -kN \ln \dfrac{NK}{V^\mu}$.

The form proposed by Boltzmann for a definition of entropy within the kinetic theory of gases has, in spite of its great merits, also certain *disadvantages*, even from the point of view of classical physics. They have been pointed out repeatedly. We shall discuss two of them in greater detail, because they are relevant for our later discussions in Part II. The first disadvantage consists in the fact that S_B depends upon a cell system. This cell system is not determined by the state of g at t or by its D^{prec}, i.e. the values u_{ij} of the magnitudes ϕ_j for the elements a_i; it is rather chosen arbitrarily. Even for the same number K of cells, different locations and different directions of the cells may be chosen. A different choice, even with the same K, leads in general to a different value of S_B for the same given D^{prec}. And the choice of K, which determines also the size $v^\mu = V^\mu/K$ of every cell, presents an insoluble dilemma. If we choose a small K and hence large cells, the determination of S_B will be imprecise, because any differences in the density of phase points *within* the cells are neglected. If we subdivide the cells and thus take $K' > K$, we obtain in general another (greater) value of S_B, which is more precise (see the example (3-34) for S^*.) It might seem not implausible to assume that, at least theoretically on the basis of the classical conception, it would be possible to increase at will the precision of the determination of S for a given D^{prec} by taking a sufficiently high K, in other words sufficiently small cells. One might perhaps even think that S could be defined theoretically, though not obtained actually, by the limit for $v^{\mu} \to 0$. [Perhaps Boltzmann himself thought so. At one place (pp. 45 f.) he tries to justify his procedure of writing differentials '$d\xi$' etc. instead of finite intervals of the coordinates and volume differentials in the phase space instead of finite volumes for the cells. However, his reasoning at this point is not very clear; and at the end of the discussion he says explicitly, that the use of differential equations in an atomistic theory can only be regarded as an approximation.] However, first of all there is no such convergence; the numerical density $f_i = N_i/v^{\mu}$ with decreasing v^{μ} becomes either 0 or grows beyond any bound; there is no positive finite limit. Secondly, a cell system with a too large K and hence very small though still positive v^{μ}, is unsuitable for Boltzmann's definition of S_B. In such a system, differences in the degree of disorder and hence differences in the thermodynamical entropy S_{th} are no longer represented by corresponding differences in the cell numbers N_i and in S_B. This becomes clear by the following examples. For simplicity, we disregard the momentum components and therefore identify the cells with spatial cells in the container of the gas. We consider two gas states G_1 and G_2 (see the examples in figs. 1 and 2). The vessel containing the gas is divided by a wall into two parts A and B. In G_1 all molecules are uniformly distributed in part A. Therefore there is a considerable difference between the densities in the two parts. This difference could be exploited to gain mechanical energy from the gas. It is clear that S_{th} in a situation of this kind is low. On the other hand, in G_2 there is uniform density throughout the container and hence high S_{th}. We form two D^{st} for G_1, D_1 and D'_1, with two different cell systems. D_1 uses $K = 2N$ small cells. Each of the N cells in part A contains one molecule. D'_1 uses $K' = K/m = 2N/m$ large cells (where m is an even number and N is divisible by m), each cell comprising m of the cells in D_1. (In the diagrams,

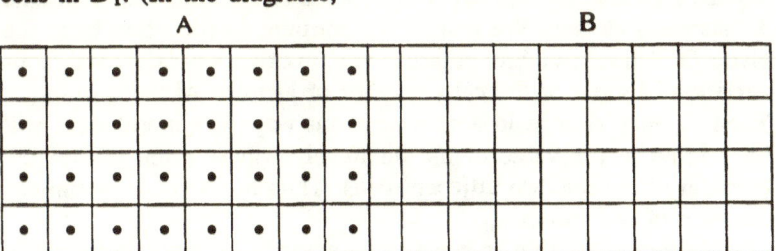

Figure. 1. Gas state G_1: all molecules in Part A.

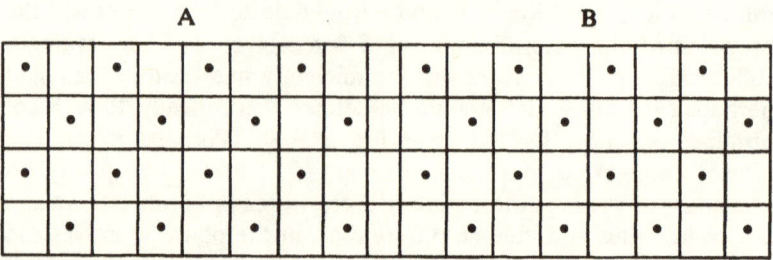

Figure. 2. Gas state G_2: uniform distribution.

we take for simplicity very small numbers: $N = 32$, $m = 4$; the $K = 64$ small cells are represented by the small squares; the $K' = 16$ large cells are indicated by heavy lines.) Let the size of the small cells be $v^\mu = 1$; then that of the large cells is $v^{\mu'} = m$. We obtain by (4-4)(a) $H(D_1) = 0$, $H(D'_1) = \dfrac{N}{m} \cdot m \ln m - N \ln m = 0$. G_2 is likewise described by two D^{st}, D_2 and D'_2 with the same cell systems as D_1 and D'_1, respectively. In D_2, just as in D_1, all cell numbers are 1 or 0; therefore $H(D_2) = H(D_1)$ and, with (4-6), $S_B(D_2) = S_B(D_1) = 0$. Thus D_1 and D_2 have equal values of S_B in spite of the great difference in the thermodynamic situation between G_1 and G_2. On the other hand, in D'_2, all cell numbers are $m/2$. Therefore $H(D'_2) = \dfrac{2N}{m} \cdot \dfrac{m}{2} \ln \dfrac{m}{2} - N \ln m = N \ln 2$. Hence $S_B(D'_2) = kN \ln 2 > S_B(D'_1)$. Thus D'_1 and D'_2 reflect the difference in S_{th} because they use a system of larger cells.

Generally speaking, K should be chosen sufficiently small to make the mean cell number N/K considerably greater than 1; in other words, K should be considerably smaller than N. (In our example, in D_1 and D_2 $N/K = 1/2$, and in D'_1 and D'_2 $N/K = 2$, which is actually still too small.)

The second disadvantage of Boltzmann's definition is perhaps even more serious from the point of view of classical physics. We assume now that for a given D^{prec}, a fixed cell system with a suitable K has been chosen. We consider a continuous transition from the given D^{prec} into a slightly different one, in other words, a continuous variation of some of the values u_{ij} (or of just one of them, say u_{11}). Then S_B may change in a discontinuous way; in general there will be a jump in the value of S_B whenever a phase point crosses the boundary between two adjacent cells. Thus S_B is not a continuous function of the values u_{ij}.

It seems desirable to construct a statistical concept S in such a way that the two disadvantageous features of S_B are avoided, in other words, such that the following two requirements are fulfilled:

(4-15) First requirement. S should not be dependent upon the arbitrary choice of a cell system.

(4-16) Second requirement. $S(D^{\text{prec}})$ should be a continuous function of the values u_{ij} in D^{prec}. The abstract concept S^{**} to be defined in Part II will fulfill these two requirements.

5
Boltzmann's H-theorem

Summary. Boltzmann stated his H-theorem as a statistical counterpart to the second law of thermodynamics. It is based on certain assumptions which are plausible but not strictly proved. Boltzmann's S_B is in agreement with thermodynamic entropy S_{th} under the condition of (approximate, local) equilibrium.

The second law of thermodynamics, the entropy principle, says that in an isolated system, e.g., a gas body enclosed in adiabatic walls, the thermodynamic entropy S_{th} always increases. (The entropy may remain constant if the process is reversible; this, however, is only an ideal case which can be approximated but not exactly realized.) If g is an isolated system, the total energy E remains constant:

(5-1) $$E(g, t_1) = E(g, t_2).$$

As a statistical counterpart to the second law, Boltzmann derived the following result by a detailed analysis of the changes in the value of H due to collisions of molecules and other processes.

(5-2) *Boltzmann's H-theorem.* Let D_1^{st} and D_2^{st} be two S^{st} describing the states of an isolated gas body g with constant energy E at the times t_1 and $t_2(>t_1)$ respectively. Suppose that $H(D_1^{st})$ is considerably higher than the mean of H for the given E. Then with overwhelming probability $H(D_2^{st}) < H(D_1^{st})$, and hence $S_B(D_2^{st}) > S_B(D_1^{st})$.

This means that in the course of time H will with great probability decrease until it is near its mean, which is very close to its minimum. Hence S_B will with great probability increase until it is near its mean, which is very close to its maximum (for the given E).

Boltzmann's derivation of his theorem was supplemented and refined by later authors. However, it is now generally recognized that the derivation does not constitute a rigorous proof. It consists rather in showing (1) that it seems plausible to assume that certain factors in the situation cancel each other out on the average for a large number of cases, and (2) that if they do, H decreases. We shall later (in §9) make some remarks about the unproved assumptions involved.

Suppose that for an isolated body of gas the total energy E, the total mass M, and the number of molecules N are known. Then the

EXAMINATION OF THE STATISTICAL CONCEPT OF ENTROPY

mass m of each molecule is $m = M/N$. For any molecule in a given cell Q_j, its momentum and hence, with m, its kinetic energy ε_j is known. We consider the simplest case, that of a diluted monatomic gas; here E is the sum of the kinetic energies of the molecules. Therefore only those D^{st} (with the given N and K) are possible which fulfill the following "energy condition":

(5-3) $$\sum_j N_j \varepsilon_j = E.$$

Among these D^{st}, let D' with cell numbers N'_j be the one for which S_B has its maximum (or its mean, which makes practically no difference) for the given E. Then the N'_j show the Maxwell-Boltzmann distribution:

(5-4) $$N'_j = e^{-\alpha - \beta \varepsilon_j},$$

where the parameters α and β are uniquely determined by $\sum N_j = N$ and (5-3). In this case the temperature T and the pressure p have the same value throughout the gas; hence the gas is in *thermodynamic equilibrium*. Therefore the distribution (5-4) of the N_j is said to characterize *statistical equilibrium*. The values of p and T are connected with the parameter β as follows:

(5-5) $$p = \frac{N}{\beta V},$$

where V is the volume of the gas body. Hence, with the gas law

(5-6) $pV = NkT$, where k is Boltzmann's constant, we obtain:

(5-7) $$T = \frac{1}{k\beta}.$$

In the case of a diluted monatomic gas, we have

(5-8) $$E = \frac{3}{2} NkT.$$

Thus the distribution (5-4) can also be expressed in the following forms, with 'C' = '$e^{-\alpha}$':

(5-9) (a) $N'_j = Ce^{-\frac{\varepsilon_j}{kT}}$,

(b) $\quad\quad = Ce^{-\frac{3N}{2E}\varepsilon_j}$.

Now we can formulate more precisely the conditions for an *agreement between Boltzmann's S_B and thermodynamic entropy S_{th}*. First, S_{th} is defined only for a state of the gas in which there is at least approximate thermodynamic equilibrium either in the whole or at least locally, i.e., in each spatial part. If the gas is in such a state, the numbers N_j and hence S_B still undergo rapid fluctuations. Therefore the agreement cannot possibly exist at all moments. The second condition is that we take the description D' with the numbers N'_j given by (5-4) or (5-9). This is a typical D^{st} (in the sense explained in §4); its S_B-value is the mean for any sufficiently long time interval. The agreement holds for this S_B, which is given by:

(5-10) $\qquad S_B(D') = -k[\sum (N'_j \ln N'_j) - N \ln v^u]$.

S_{th} is defined in classical physics only up to an arbitrary additive constant. Under the conditions mentioned, S_B and S_{th} are numerically equal if the constant is suitably chosen.

Suppose that the vessel containing the gas g is divided by adiabatic walls into several parts. Suppose further that, at the given time, for each part g_n of g the two conditions are fulfilled: that is to say, g_n is in or near to thermodynamic equilibrium and we take a corresponding D^{st} for g_n which is nearly in statistical equilibrium. Then the agreement between S_B and S_{th} holds for each part g_n. Now the value of S_{th} for the whole gas body is equal to the sum of its values for the parts, and S_B is likewise additive (4-11). Therefore the agreement holds also for the whole.

In order to obtain a model for a process in which the entropy increases toward its maximum, we again consider the vessel divided into parts, with thermodynamic equilibrium in each part; T and p may have different values, high in some parts, lower in others. But now we perforate each wall by a hole so small that the equalization of T and p takes place very slowly. Then at any time t during this process, there is still approximate thermodynamic equilibrium in each part. And if again we take at any t the typical D^s, i.e., the combination of typical D^{st} for the parts, we have still agreement between S_B and S_{th}. According to the second law, S_{th} increases during the process until it reaches its maximum. And according to Boltzmann's H-theorem, S_B does likewise.

6
The Problem of the Definition of Entropy for other than Statistical Descriptions

Summary. With this section, the critical examination of the statistical concept of entropy begins. Boltzmann applied his concept S_B only to D^{st}. Later physicists extended its use to other descriptions, including D^{ind}. We discuss two basically different methods for this extension, which we call Methods I and II. First, we state two principles which seem to be generally accepted (tacitly) for any purely physical magnitude M (as distinguished from other, e.g., logical or epistemological concepts): (1) If M is a function of certain parameters, and two descriptions state the same values for these parameters, then we must ascribe to M the same value on the basis of either description (6-1); (2) if M has the same value on the basis of each of several descriptions, then it has also the same value on the basis of their disjunction (6-2). Method I, which I advocate, defines the extended concept S_B^I in such a way that the two principles are fulfilled; therefore S_B^I is a purely physical concept. For a D^{st}, S_B^I has the same value as S_B. For a D^{prec} or a D^{ind}, S_B^I has the same value as for the corresponding D^{st}. If each of several D^{st} has the same value of S_B, then this is also the value of S_B^I for their disjunction. It is shown that S_B^I for any of these descriptions is in accord with S_{th}. In Method II, an extended concept S_B^{II} is defined for any description D_i in such a way that its value is, aside from an additive constant, proportional to the logarithm of the probability of D_i (where, in accordance with Boltzmann's conception, all D^{ind} are taken as equally probable). It seems that this concept S_B^{II} is customarily accepted by physicists. However, it is shown that S_B^{II}, in contrast to S_B^I, is not generally in accord with thermodynamic entropy except for a D^{st}. It violates the two principles and therefore is not a purely physical concept; it is even a purely logical concept. Therefore it is entirely out of line with Boltzmann's aim to construct a physical, statistical concept corresponding to the thermodynamic concept of entropy.

Boltzmann's concept of entropy S_B was originally applied by himself and other physicists only to statistical descriptions (or the states described by them). The way in which Boltzmann and others talk about "the state" of a gas g at a given time t as described by a D^{st} suggests that perhaps a D^{st} more than a D^{ind} appears to them as representing "the objective physical reality." However, on the basis of the classical conception, the objective state in its quantitative aspects is the set of the actual values of the magnitudes ϕ_j; hence its representation is a D^{prec} rather than a D^{st}. Once a cell system Ω is chosen, a given D_i^{prec} determines uniquely the corresponding D_i^{ind} and the corresponding D_i^{st}. While D_i^{ind} is still an approximation of D_i^{prec}, D_i^{st} is a very weak consequence of D_i^{ind} and therefore a very limited description of the state, although very useful for certain purposes.

After the time of Boltzmann, physicists applied the concept S_B also to other kinds of descriptions, including D^{ind}. But the question whether and how this extension is to be made seems still controversial. Or rather, there seems to be a lack of explicit agreement without controversy. At least, I have not seen so far any discussion in print concerning the possible modes of extension. Usually the extension is made tacitly, without an explicit formulation of a definition; still less are reasons given for the choice of the method.

We shall explain two quite different methods of extension for S_B. But first a brief remark about the view that S_B must be restricted to D^{st} and that any extension of it and, in particular, any application to D^{ind} is illegitimate. (I have not found this view in print, but only in conversations.) I find it hard to understand on what reasons this view might be based; it seems to me to give to the concept S_B a peculiar role by permitting it to violate the subsequent principle (6-1)(A). On the basis of the conception of classical physics, this principle seems to be tacitly assumed for any ordinary, purely physical measurable magnitude M.

(6-1) *Principle of physical magnitudes.* Let M be a physical magnitude applicable to the state of a physical system s at time t with respect to a reference system R. Let M be defined in terms of n other magnitudes $m_1, \ldots, m_n$; i.e., if the values of these magnitudes are given (with a certain precision) then the value of M is thereby uniquely determined (with a certain precision). Let D_1 and D_2 be two descriptions of s at a specified time t_0 with respect to R such that D_1 and D_2 give the same values of $m_1(s, t_0), \ldots, m_n(s, t_0)$. If M is defined in such a way that, on the basis of D_1, a certain value x is ascribed to M for s at t_0 with respect to R, then:
(A) on the basis of D_2, a value should be ascribed to M,
(B) this value must be equal to x.

Part (A) of the principle is not satisfied by the conception of S_B mentioned above. Part (B) will be used later as an argument for my Method I as against the customary Method II.

Example. Suppose that s is a straight rigid bar, which at time t_0 is at rest in the spatial coordinate system R. D_1 gives the six spatial coordinates of the two end points of the bar at time t_0 with respect to R. D_2 gives the same values of the coordinates, but adds that s is made of copper and that its temperature at t_0 is 100°C. Let M be the length of s at t_0 with respect to R. Here it seems obvious that on the basis of D_2 the same value must be ascribed to M as on D_1. But now suppose that M' is a new magnitude proposed by a physicist. He defines it in such a way that its value for s at t with respect to R on the basis of descriptions like D_1 is determined by a function f of the six coordinates mentioned; hence on D_1, the value of M' is equal to the value of f for the coordinate values stated in D_1. Although the author of a new concept is certainly free to decide how to define it, within the context of classical physics most physicists would find it strange if the author declared that on D_2 no value should be ascribed to M'. And if he constructed the definition in such a way that M' had a value on D_2, but not the same as the value on D_1, then many physicists would say that M' is not a purely physical concept; it might be a logical concept dependent on the logical properties of the description D in question, or an epistemological concept dependent on the state of knowledge of an observer as formulated in D. Or again, it might be a concept of a mixed nature, dependent on both physical and non-physical, say logical or epistemological, data.

These considerations suggest that the decision concerning the application of S_B to descriptions of other kinds will depend upon the general nature and purpose of the statistical concept of entropy.

The concept of entropy in thermodynamics (S_{th}) had the same general character as the other concepts in the same field, e.g., temperature, heat, energy, pressure, etc. It served, just like these other concepts, for the quantitative characterization of some objective property of a state of a physical system, say, the gas g in the container in the laboratory at the time t. When the kinetic theory of gases was developed, one of the essential problems was to find counterparts to the thermodynamic concepts within this theory, to be defined in terms of statistical mechanics. Thus Boltzmann's problem was not essentially different from the analogous problems for the other concepts. As, for example, the statistical equivalent of temperature was found to be proportional to the mean kinetic energy of the molecules, Boltzmann found that the statistical equivalent of entropy was a certain logarithmic function of the cell numbers. It is true that the situation with respect to entropy differs in one respect from that of the other concepts: Boltzmann introduced as a new constituent the cell system, which is not determined by the objective state of the physical system itself, but must be chosen arbitrarily. However, this fact, although not unimportant, does not mark a fundamental difference in the general character of the concept. First, if the number of cells is made sufficiently large, then under ordinary conditions as in a gas the influence of a change of the cell system is numerically small. And secondly, it is possible to modify the Boltzmann concept in such a way that the arbitrary cell system disappears; this will be shown later (in Part II). Therefore it seems to me that the statistical concept of entropy introduced by Boltzmann was meant by him as a purely physical concept just like the original thermodynamic concept of entropy.

The following principle (6-2) seems likewise to be generally accepted by tacit convention for any purely physical concept.

(6-2) *Principle of disjunction.* Let M be a physical magnitude. Suppose that, for a given physical system at a given time with respect to a given reference system R, M has the same value on the basis of each of several descriptions. Then H has the same value also on the basis of the disjunction of these descriptions.

Example. Let M be the length of a bar s at time t_0 in R, as in the previous example. Let s be parallel to the x-axis. Let the x-coordinates of the endpoints of s at t_0 be stated in D_1 as 1.3 and 1.5, in D_2 as 2.3 and 2.5, and in D_3 as 3.3 and 3.5. Thus $M(D_1) = M(D_2) = M(D_3) = 0.2$. The principle of disjunction says that on the basis of the disjunction D_d of the three descriptions, M is likewise 0.2.

Assume again that M' is a new magnitude proposed by a physicist. Suppose that his definition of M' is such that, on the basis of each of the descriptions D_1, D_2, and D_3, $M' = 0.2$. He is certainly free to construct his definition as he sees fit, as long as it is consistent. Suppose that definition is such that, on the basis of the disjunction D_d, it leads to a value of M' different from 0.2. We cannot say that the definition is inconsistent; but again, as in the previous example, many physicists would say that M' is then not a purely physical concept.

Both principles seem rather obvious. They may even appear to the reader as too obvious and trivial to bother about their explicit formulation. However, we shall find that the customary form of the concept of entropy in statistical mechanics violates both principles.

Now we shall explain the alternative Methods I and II for extending the definitions of H and S_B. We denote the concepts resulting from Method I by 'H^I' and 'S_B^I' and those from Method II by 'H^{II}' and 'S_B^{II}.'

The main characteristic of *Method I*, which I advocate, is the conception of H and S_B as purely physical concepts. Consequently, the concepts H^I and S_B^I will be defined in such a way that they satisfy the principles (6-1) and (6-2). Let a D^{st} for g at t be given, say D_1^{st}. It is based on a space-time coordinate system and a system Ω^μ of K cells in the μ-space; these two systems together constitute the reference system R in the principle (6-1). $H(D^{st})$ is a function of the cell numbers $N_1, \ldots, N_K$ ($N = \sum N_j$, K is given by R, k is a universal constant with respect to R). Thus these cell numbers are in this case the magnitudes m_1, etc. referred to in the principle. Let D_2 be another description of any kind for g at t with respect to R which states the same cell numbers N_j as D_1^{st}. Then, according to the principle (6-1), the definition of H is to be extended in such a way that

(6-3) $$H^I(D_2) = H(D_1^{st}).$$

We define S_B^I in analogy to (4-6), but now for any description D_i to which H^I is applicable:

(6-4) $$S_B^I(D_i) =_{Df} -kH^I(D_i).$$

Then S_B^I will likewise satisfy (6-1).

In order to fulfil (6-3), we define

(6-5) $H^I(D_i^{ind}) =_{Df} H(D_i^{st})$, where D_i^{st} is the D^{st} corresponding to D_i^{ind}.

Hence with (6-4):

(6-6) $$S_B^I(D_i^{ind}) = -kH(D_i^{st}) = S_B(D_i^{st}).$$

Let $D_i^{d\text{-ind}}$ be a disjunction of several D^{ind} which correspond to the same D_i^{st} and therefore have the same value of S_B^I. In order to fulfil the principle of disjunction, we assign to $D_i^{d\text{-ind}}$ likewise this value of S_B^I:

(6-7) $$S_B^I(D_i^{d\text{-ind}}) =_{Df} S_B(D_i^{st}).$$

Let $D_i^{d\text{-st}}$ be a disjunction of several D^{st}, including D_i^{st}, which have the same value of S_B as D_i^{st}. Again, in order to fulfil the principle of disjunction, we assign the same value also to the disjunction:

(6-8) $$S_B^I(D_i^{d\text{-st}}) =_{Df} S_B(D_i^{st}).$$

We can extend the definition of H^I also to a D^{prec} in accordance with (6-3). In this case, however, we must insert into the definiendum a reference to a cell system Ω^μ, because a D^{prec}, in contradistinction to a D^{st} or a D^{ind}, does itself not refer to a cell system:

(6-9) $H^I(D_i^{prec}, \Omega^\mu) =_{Df} H(D_i^{st})$, where Ω^μ is any cell system and D_i^{st} is that D^{st} based on Ω^μ which corresponds to D_i^{prec} (i.e., is logically implied by it). Hence with (6-4):

(6-10) $$S_B^I(D_i^{prec}, \Omega^\mu) = S_B(D_i^{st}).$$

Let us examine the relation between S_B^I and thermodynamic entropy S_{th}. Suppose that g at time t_1 is in a state of near-equilibrium and that D_1^{st} is a typical description of g at t_1. Then $S_B^I(D_1^{st}) = S_B(D_1^{st}) = S_{th}(g, t_1)$. Then, for any D^{ind} corresponding to D_1^{st}, for any disjunction of several D^{ind} of this kind, and for any D^{prec} corresponding to D_1^{st} (with respect to the cell system used in D_1^{st}), the value of S_B^I is equal to $S_B(D_1^{st})$ and hence to $S_{th}(g, t_1)$. Furthermore, let D_i be a disjunction of several D^{st}, including D_1^{st}, each of which has the same S_B-value as D_1^{st}. Then $S_B^I(D_i) = S_B(D_1^{st}) = S_{th}(g, t_1)$. Thus *the value of S_B^I for any of these descriptions is in accord with S_{th}*.

Our earlier extension of the concept S^* (for a simple classification, cf. §3) to D^{ind} (see (3-31)) was likewise in accordance with Method I.

Method II, which seems to be most frequently used when an extension of S_B is made proceeds as follows. For a given system of N molecules and a given system Ω^μ of K cells, let D_i be a disjunction of m distinct D^{ind} ($1 \leq m \leq Z = K^N$; the cell numbers need not be the same in the several components of D_i). Method II is characterized by defining $H^{II}(D_i)$ by a function of the form $-\ln m +$ const., and hence $S_B^{II}(D_i)$ by $k(\ln m - \text{const.})$. The constant is chosen in various ways, sometimes as 0. Let us take it in such a form that S_B^{II} is in accordance with S_B in the case of a D^{st}. Therefore we define:

(6-11) (a) $\quad S_B^{II}(D_i) =_{Df} k\left\{\ln m - N \ln \dfrac{NK}{V^\mu}\right\}$

(b) $\quad\quad\quad = k[\ln m - N \ln N + N \ln V^\mu]$.

Any D_i^{st} is logically equivalent to the disjunction of the z corresponding D^{ind}.

Therefore

$$(6\text{-}12) \qquad S_B^{II}(D_i^{st}) = k\left\{\ln z(D_i^{st}) - N \ln \frac{NK}{V^\mu}\right\}.$$

As we see from (4-5)(a) and (4-6), this is indeed equal to $S_B(D_i^{st})$ (with the approximation (3-9)(b), which is always used in statistical mechanics); hence S_B^{II} is indeed an extension of Boltzmann's concept S_B.

For a D^{ind}, $m = 1$. Therefore:

$$(6\text{-}13) \qquad S_B^{II}(D_i^{ind}) = -kN \ln \frac{NK}{V^\mu}.$$

For the concept S^* (§3), we defined an extension S^{*I} in (3-31), which applies Method I. A definition of S^{*II}, which applies Method II, will be given later in (10-15).

For Boltzmann's probability distribution pr_B (4-8), we have:

$$(6\text{-}14) \qquad pr_B(D_i) = \frac{m}{Z},$$

where $Z = K^N$. Therefore $\ln pr_B(D_i) - \ln m - N \ln K$. Hence

$$(6\text{-}15) \qquad S_B^{II}(D_i) = k\left\{\ln pr_B(D_i) - N \ln \frac{N}{V^\mu}\right\}.$$

Sometimes S_B^{II} is directly defined in terms of probability in the form $k(\ln pr_B(D_i) - \text{const.})$, e.g., by (6-15) or with const. $= 0$. We see that the simple relation between S_B and pr_B (4-10), which for our form S_B^I holds only in the case of D^{st}, holds for S_B^{II} generally with any D_i of the kind described, including all D^{ind}. This result—and another related result concerning the amount of information (§10)—may at first glance appear as an advantage of Method II in comparison with I; and it was perhaps the main motivation for those who accepted Method II.

However, Method II has also very serious disadvantages. We shall show that S_B^{II} is in most cases not in agreement with thermodynamic entropy S_{th}. Moreover, S_B^{II} is not a purely physical concept but a purely logical concept. This will become clear by the consideration of some examples.

The *first two examples* use a simple case of the model explained in §5. The vessel containing the gas g is divided by a wall into two parts A and B. During a time interval around t_1 long enough for repeated measurements, it is found that the temperature throughout part A remains T_A, and throughout B T_B; similarly the pressure throughout A remains p_A, and throughout B p_B, where $T_A > T_B > 0$ and $p_A > p_B > 0$. Later the wall is removed and a process of equalization of T and p takes place. During a still later interval around t_2, T is found to have the value T_2 and p the value p_2 throughout the vessel. Then, according to the second law:

$$(6\text{-}16) \qquad S_{\text{th}}(g, t_2) > S_{\text{th}}(g, t_1).$$

Let D_A^{st} be a typical D^{st} for part A and D_B^{st} for part B for the first time period. Let D_1^{st} be the combination of D_A^{st} and D_B^{st}; thus D_1^{st} is a typical D^{st} for the whole gas for the first period. Let D_2^{st} be typical for the second period. Then we see from the discussion in the preceding section:

(6-17) (a) $S_B(D_1^{\text{st}}) = S_{\text{th}}(g, t_1)$,

(b) $S_B(D_2^{\text{st}}) = S_{\text{th}}(g, t_2)$;

and

$$(6\text{-}18) \qquad S_B(D_2^{\text{st}}) > S_B(D_1^{\text{st}}),$$

in accordance with Boltzmann's H-theorem.

Example 1. We have assumed D_1^{st} and D_2^{st} to be true (typical descriptions of g at t_1 and t_2, respectively. Now let D_1^{ind} be the one true D^{ind} corresponding to D_1^{st}, and likewise D_2^{ind} for D_2^{st}. (Although no observer can know which of the D^{ind} is the true one, we can, within the conception of classical physics, refer to it hypothetically, just as we can refer to the unknown value u_1 of a magnitude u at time t_1.) If $z(D_i^{\text{st}})$ were $= 1$, then all molecules would be concentrated in a very small part of the vessel. Since this is not the case in D_1^{st}, we have $z(D_1^{\text{st}}) > 1$. Therefore, with (6-13) and (6-12):

$$(6\text{-}19) \qquad S_B^{\text{II}}(D_2^{\text{ind}}) = S_B^{\text{II}}(D_1^{\text{ind}}) < S_B(D_1^{\text{st}}).$$

EXAMINATION OF THE STATISTICAL CONCEPT OF ENTROPY 41

Hence with (6-17)(a) and (6-16):

(6-20) $\quad S_B^{II}(D_2^{ind}) = S_B^{II}(D_1^{ind}) < S_{th}(g, t_1) < S_{th}(g, t_2).$

Thus we see that S_B^{II} has the same value for D_1^{ind} and D_2^{ind}, a value that is smaller than S_{th} for t_1 and still smaller than S_{th} for t_2. This shows that S_B^{II} is not in accord with S_{th}. D_1^{ind} is not only a true description of the state of the gas at t_1 but a description from which D_1^{st} is deducible, which in turn yields the value $S_B(D_1^{st})$ which agrees with $S_{th}(g, t_1)$; the situation for D_2^{ind} is analogous. Thus we see that, although D_1^{ind} and D_2^{ind} contain the relevant information for the determination of correct S-values (i.e., those which agree with S_{th}), S_B^{II} assigns to them other values. More generally, we see from (6-13) that S_B^{II} has the same value for *all* D^{ind} (for given V^u, K, and N), although these D^{ind} describe all possible states of g with a great variation in S_B, in S_{th}, and hence in the amount of available energy which could be transformed into mechanical work. *Thus S_B^{II} for D^{ind} has no connection whatever with thermodynamic entropy and available energy.* Since $S_B^{II}(D_1^{ind}) < S_B^{II}(D_1^{st})$, S_B^{II} violates the principle (6-1)(B). *Therefore S_B^{II} is not a purely physical concept.*

Example 2. We use again D_1^{st} and D_2^{st} as described above. It follows from (6-18) that $z(D_2^{st}) > z(D_1^{st})$. Let us suppose now that the differences $T_A - T_B$ and $p_A - p_B$ are small (one of them may even be 0) but at least one of them is still noticeable, so that the results of the measurements still lead to (6-16). Then $z(D_2^{st})$ is not very much greater than $z(D_1^{st})$. Let n be a positive integer (say the smallest one) such that

(6-21) $\quad n \times z(D_1^{st}) > z(D_2^{st}).$

Now let D_1^d be a disjunction of n D^{st} which have the same z as D_1^{st}. Then D_1^d is logically equivalent to a disjunction of $n \times z(D_1^{st})$ D^{ind}. Therefore, with (6-21) and (6-11):

(6-22) $\quad S_B^{II}(D_1^d) > S_B^{II}(D_2^{st}).$

Hence with (6-17)(b):

(6-23) $\quad S_B^{II}(D_1^d) > S_{th}(g, t_2).$

The n D^{st} in D_1^d may be typical D^{st} for states of g similar to that in the period around t_1; only the wall between the parts A and B is in different positions, while the volumes of A and B and the values of T_A, T_B, p_A, and p_B are the same in all cases. Then D_1^d says that g is in one of n states which have the same value of S_B, equal to $S_B(D_1^{st})$, hence $< S_B(D_2^{st})$, and the same value of S_{th}, equal to $S_{th}(g, t_1)$, hence $< S_{th}(g, t_2)$. Thus it follows from D_1^d that the S_{th} of g is smaller than $S_{th}(g, t_2)$; on the other hand, S_B^{II} is greater than for D_2^{st} (6-22), and greater than $S_{th}(g, t_2)$ (6-23). In this case, *the inequality between the values of S_B^{II} (6-22) is the inverse of that between the values of S_{th}*.

We found that S_B^{II} is not a purely physical concept. Now it is easy to see that it is not even a mixed concept with a physical component, but a purely logical concept. This is shown by the following example.

Example 3. Suppose we know that the gas g was in a state of thermodynamic equilibrium during a time interval around t_1; we know the volume of the vessel and the volumes of the parts separated by walls, the number N of molecules and the numbers for the parts, and the molecular mass m; furthermore, a cell system Ω^μ with V^μ and K is specified. Now let us consider various descriptions; they are meant as typical descriptions of g for the interval around t_1.

(3a) Suppose that D_1^{st} is given to us. Then we can calculate the value of $S_B(D_1^{st})$, say r_1 (a particular real number), and we can infer that S_{th} is likewise $= r_1$.

(3b) Suppose that instead of D_1^{st} we obtain only the statement "$S_B = r_1$." This means: "The (unspecified) D^{st} for g at t_1 is such that its S_B is r_1," because the (unextended) concept S_B applies only to D^{st}. From this statement we can still infer that $S_{th} = r_1$.

(3c) Suppose we are told: "$S_B^I = r_1$." S_B^I is applicable to any description giving a set of cell numbers N_j or a common value of S_B for several D^{st}, and the value of S_B^I for such a description is equal to the corresponding value of $S_B(D^{st})$. Therefore the present statement means the same as that in (3b).

(3d) Now we consider, in contrast, the situation with S_B^{II}. Let the statement "$S_B^{II} = r_1'$" be given, with a specified real number r_1'. S_B^{II} is defined for any disjunction D_m of m D^{ind} with any m ($1 \leq m \leq Z$). Therefore the given statement means: "There is a number m and an (unspecified) D_m which holds for g at t_1 and for which $S_B^{II} = r_1'$." Now we see from (6-11) that, since k is known and

V^μ, K, and N are supposed to be given, S_B^{II} depends merely on m; and conversely from the given S_B^{II}-value r_1', we can determine the value of m, say m_1 $\left[\text{viz., } m_1 = e^{r_1'/k}\left(\dfrac{NK}{V^\mu}\right)^N\right]$. Suppose we find $m_1 = 1000$. Then the given statement means: "There is a disjunction of one thousand D^{ind} which holds for g at t_1." The statement does not tell us *which* D^{ind} belong to the disjunction; it says nothing about the content of these D^{ind}, the cell numbers or anything else. It says merely that the (unspecified) disjunction consists of one thousand D^{ind}; this is a logical characteristic concerning logical strength or amount of information. The statement can also be formulated in this way: "The one (unspecified) D^{ind} which holds for g at t_1 belongs to an (unspecified) class of one thousand D^{ind}." This holds obviously for every D^{ind} and for every possible state of g. It is a tautology, a purely logical truth. Therefore S_B^{II} *is a purely logical concept*. If it is to be introduced at all, the term "entropy" should not be used for it.

(3e) The situation is quite similar, if the statement "$S_B^{II'} = r_1'$" is given, where $S_B^{II'}$ is defined in terms of pr_B (see the earlier remark on (6-15)). From the given statement we can determine the probability of an (unspecified) description which holds for g at t_1, say $pr_B = 0.0001$. Thus what we learn about g at t_1 is merely that its state can truly be described by an (unspecified) description which has the probability 0.0001. But this again holds for any possible state of the gas.

The strangeness of the results to which Method II leads becomes especially striking in the following case.

Example 4. Let D_1^S assign to g at t_1 a value of S_B with a certain precision, by specifying a small interval on the S_B-scale. We take again the D_1^{st} of Examples 1 and 2. D_1^{st} was assumed to be typical for g at t_1. To make the example more concrete, let us assume that

(6-24) $$S_B(D_1^{st}) = -10^7 k.$$

Let D_1^S say that the mean S_B for the period around t_1 is $-10^7 k \pm \delta$. Then D_1^S is equivalent to a disjunction of certain D^{st}, namely those whose S_B-values lie within the given interval, among them D_1^{st}. Since each D^{st} is a disjunction of certain D^{ind}, D_1^S is equivalent to a disjunction of a great number of D^{ind}, say m. Suppose that the size 2δ of the interval is such that $m = Z/10^6$; thus the interval covers one millionth of the number of all D^{ind}. Then $pr_B(D_1^S) = 10^{-6}$. So far we did not specify either V^μ or N; let us assume for simplicity that they happen to be equal. Then from (6-15), $S_B^{II}(D_1^S) = k \ln pr_B(D_1^S) = -13.8k$. Since S_B^{II} claims to be a concept of entropy and simply an extension of S_B, the result obtained may be formulated as follows:

(6-25) "The entropy (S_B^{II}) of the gas g at t_1 on the basis of the description D_1^S, which says that the entropy (S_B) of g at t_1 is near to $-10,000,000k$, is $-13.8k$."

This result is, to say the least, rather strange. D_1^{st} was assumed to be a typical description of g for the specified period. Hence the mean value of S_B for g during the period is $-10^7 k$. According to (6-17) (a), this is then also the value of S_{th}. D_1^S is likewise true; but the value of S_B^{II} for D_1^S is $-13.8k$. Obviously this value has no relation at all to thermodynamic entropy.

The application of Method I leads in this example to the only plausible result, which is here not a point value but an interval. D_1^S is a disjunction of certain D_i^{st}. For each of them, $S_B^I(D_i^{st}) = S_B(D_i^{st})$, and likewise, according to (6-8), for any partial disjunction consisting of D^{st} which have the same S_B-value as D_i^{st}. The D^{st} contained in D_1^S are those for which S_B is in the interval $-10^7 k \pm \delta$; therefore S_B^I determines for D_1^S just this interval.

The analyses in this section have shown the following. If the extension of S_B is intended to maintain the character as a physical concept in statistical mechanics which is related to the thermodynamic concept of entropy, their Method II must be rejected and Method I must be applied.

7
Gibbs's Statistical Method

Summary. The state of the whole system of N elements, e.g., the gas g, is represented by a point U in the Mn-dimensional γ-space. A description D_1 of g at t_1 is represented by the point set R_1 in the γ-space, called the range of D_1. Let the volume of R_1 be v_1. Then the (probability) density $\rho_1(U)$ based on D_1 is $1/v_1$ at any point U in R_1, and 0 outside of R_1. Let D_2 be the description of g at a later time t_2, derived from D_1 with the help of the laws of mechanics. The range of D_2 has the same volume as that of D_1 (Liouville's theorem), although a different location and shape.

The development of new method for statistical mechanics by Gibbs[1] constitutes an essential progress. We shall give a brief exposition of the essential features of his method, based chiefly on Tolman.[2] We shall, however, use some of our own terms and notations. This seems necessary because the customary formulations, both in words and in symbols, are almost always elliptical and therefore often not quite clear.

In the next section we shall explain Gibbs's definition of entropy and show that it is characterized by what we have called Method II. Then we shall indicate an alternative definition (§9) which uses instead Method I and thereby leads to a magnitude which is in accordance with the principles for purely physical concepts, (6-1) and (6-2).

In Boltzmann's method, each of the N molecules a_i of the gas g, characterized by the values of n magnitudes $u_{i1}, \ldots, u_{in}$, is represented by a phase point in the n-dimensional μ-space. Gibbs represents the state of g itself, or its description D^{prec}, which is characterized by the Nn values $u_{11}, \ldots, u_{1n}, u_{21}, \ldots, u_{2n}, \ldots, u_{N1}, \ldots, u_{Nn}$, by a phase point in the Nn-dimensional phase space, called γ-*space* (gas-space). We shall use 'U' as a variable for an ordered set of Nn values $u_{11}, \ldots, u_{Nn}$ as coordinates, and hence for a point in the γ-space. R^μ determines the total range R^γ in the γ-space; let V^γ be its (Nn-dimensional) volume ($V^\gamma = (V^\mu)^N$).

---

[1] J. W. Gibbs, *Elementary Principles in Statistical Mechanics* (New Haven; Yale University Press, 1902).

[2] Richard C. Tolman, *The Principles of Statistical Mechanics* (London: Oxford University Press, 1938), Ch. vi.

Now the main new feature of Gibbs's method is as follows. If the precise description D_1^{prec} of the gas body g at the initial time t_1 were known, the precise description D_2^{prec} of g at a later time t_2 could be determined with the help of the laws of classical mechanics. In fact, however, actual observations (or hypothetical assumptions) supply only a weaker description of g at t_1, say D_1. This description determines, not a single point, but a region in the γ-space; this we call the *range* of D_1, $R(D_1)$. Gibbs calls the class $R(D_1)$ of phase points, or the class of possible states of the gas g represented by these phase points, the representative *ensemble* of g at t_1 as described by D_1.

An ensemble is characterized in Gibbs's method by a probability density function $\rho(U)$ over the γ-space. The probability on the basis of ρ that the phase point of the gas state represented by the ensemble belongs to a region R_l is:

(7-1) $$pr(R_l) = \int_{R_l} \rho(U)\, dU.$$

('dU' is short for '$du_{11} \cdots du_{Nn}$'; the integral symbol stands for an Nn-fold integral.) Any density function ρ is normalized to 1:

(7-2) $\int \rho(U)\, dU = 1$, where the integral covers the whole γ-space.

Outside of the total range R^γ, ρ is taken to be 0. Therefore the integral (7-2) over R^γ is likewise 1. On the basis of any description D_i, the density function ρ_i based on D_i is taken to be 0 outside of $R(D_i)$. Therefore:

(7-3) $$\int_{R(D_i)} \rho_i(U)\, dU = 1.$$

Let F be a physical magnitude $F(g, t)$ of g at time t, which is defined as a function of the Nn value $u_{11}, \ldots, u_{Nn}$ for g at $t: F(u_{11}, \ldots, u_{Nn}; t)$. It may therefore be represented as a function over the γ-space: $F(U, t)$. If a density function $\rho(U, t)$ is given, the *ensemble mean* $\bar{\bar{F}}$ of F at t (in the sense of the probability mean, in other words, the expectation value) is defined as follows:

(7-4) $$\bar{\bar{F}}(g, t) =_{\text{Df}} \int F(U, t)\rho(U, t)\, dU.$$

Gibbs takes this ensemble-mean $\bar{\bar{F}}(g, t)$, based on the density function ρ for t determined by a description D_i, as the value we should reasonably expect for $F(g, t)$ if D_i represents all the data we have

EXAMINATION OF THE STATISTICAL CONCEPT OF ENTROPY 47

(or assume). In the terminology of inductive logic, this means the *estimate* of $F(g, t)$ with respect to the observational evidence D_i:

(7-5) $$\text{est}\,(F, g, t, D_i) = \bar{\bar{F}}(g, t).$$

The application of this method of estimation presupposes two postulates: (1) the laws of mechanics, (2) a probability assumption. The laws (1) are used only if the time t of the estimated value differs from the time t_i to which D_i refers; in this case the laws are needed for deriving $\rho(U, t)$ from $\rho(U, t_i)$ determined by D_i. The probability postulate is needed for the determination of $\rho(U, t_i)$ from D_i.

The following postulate is assumed, in accordance with Boltzmann's probability assumption (4-8):

(7-6) *Postulate of apriori density:*
  (a) Outside $R^\gamma, \rho = 0$.
  (b) Within R^γ, ρ is constant $= \rho_0$.

Any description of g at t in our discussions is supposed to be such that it merely excludes some possible cases, i.e., some values of the n magnitudes ϕ_j, but does not say anything about the probabilities of the nonexcluded cases. Thus it may state, for example, intervals for some of the m magnitudes or for other magnitudes defined on their basis, but it does not give a probability distribution within any of these intervals. Therefore a description D_i is completely characterized by its range R_i. Then the postulate (7-6) yields:

(7-7) *Apriori probability* pr_0 for a description D_i whose range R_i has the volume v_i:

$$pr_0(D_i) = pr_0(R_i) = \int_{R_i} \rho_0(U)\, dU = v_i \rho_0.$$

Since for a tautology, whose range is R^γ with volume V^μ, pr_0 must be 1:

(7-8) $$\rho_0 = \frac{1}{V^\mu}$$

Hence:

(7-9) $$pr_0(D_i) = pr_0(R_i) = \frac{v_i}{V^\gamma}.$$

(7-10) Rule for the *aposteriori density* $\rho_i(U, t)$ based on a description D_i for t:
   (a) Outside R_i, $\rho_i(U, t) = 0$,
   (b) Within R_i, $\rho_i(U, t)$ is constant.

Hence with (7-3):

(7-11) For any point U within R_i, $\rho_i(U, t) = \dfrac{1}{v_i}$.

The *aposteriori or relative probability* of a description D_j with range R_j on the basis of D_i, where D_i and D_j refer to the same time t, is defined as follows:

(7-12) $$pr(D_j \mid D_i) =_{Df} \int_{R_j} \rho_i(U, t)\, dU.$$

This leads to the customary form:

(7-13) $$pr(D_j \mid D_i) = \frac{pr_0(D_i \cdot D_j)}{pr_0(D_i)}.$$

Hence, if the range of the conjunction $D_i \cdot D_j$ (which is the intersection of R_i and R_j) has the volume v_{ij}:

(7-14) $$pr(D_j \mid D_i) = \frac{v_{ij}}{v_i}.$$

Let D_1 be a description of g at time t_1. Let the range of D_1 be R_1 with volume v_1. Let D_2 be the description of g at a later time t_2, as derived from D_1 according to the laws of mechanics. Let the range of D_2 be R_2 with volume v_2. We assume for D_1, but not for D_2, that it is a description not involving probability. Hence we derive from D_1 the density function $\rho_1(U)$ according to (7-10) and (7-11). The laws of mechanics determine, for a given initial phase point U_1 at t_1, the later phase point U_2 at t_2. Therefore, from the initial density function $\rho_1(U)$, the density function $\rho_2(U)$ for t_2 can be derived. With respect to this situation, the following important results (7-15) and (7-16) hold, known as *Liouville's theorem* (1838):

(7-15) $$v_1 = v_2.$$

This means that, although the range of the ensemble changes location and shape in the course of time, its volume remains unchanged.

(7-16) (a) Outside R_2, $\rho_2(U) = 0$.

(b) For every U within R_2, $\rho_2(U) = \dfrac{1}{v_2} = \dfrac{1}{v_1}$

($= \rho_1$ within R_1).

Thus ρ_2 is constant in R_2. Therefore D_2 is likewise a description not involving probability but completely characterized by its range.

8
Gibbs's Definition of Entropy for an Ensemble

Summary. On the basis of Boltzmann's cells in the μ-space, Gibbs defines cells Q^γ in the γ-space. If a "fine-grained" density $\rho_i(U)$ is given the "coarse-grained" density $P_i(Q_k^\gamma)$ is defined as the mean of ρ_i in the cell Q_k^γ. Supposedly as an analogue to Boltzmann's H, Gibbs's H_G^{II} is defined as the ensemble mean of $\ln P_i$. Gibbs's entropy concept S_G^{II} is then defined as $-kH_G^{II}$. Both concepts are applicable not only to D^{st} but to descriptions of any form. They use implicitly Method II (§6). For any D^{ind} or disjunction of several D^{ind} or any D^{st} or disjunction of D^{st}, S_G^{II} has, aside from an additive constant the same value as S_B^{II}. It is shown that S_G^{II} is in general, except for D^{st}, not in agreement with thermodynamic entropy S_{th}. Gibbs states a theorem which says that, under certain conditions, S_B^{II} increases in the course of time. It is shown that this increase has nothing to do with the increase of S_{th} and therefore Gibbs's theorem is not a statistical counterpart to the second law of thermodynamics, as it is supposed to be.

The aim of Gibbs's definition of entropy was essentially the same as that of Boltzmann's, viz., to provide a statistical concept corresponding to the thermodynamic concept of entropy S_{th}. But Gibbs's concept is based on his new statistical method and is therefore defined with respect to ensembles in the γ-space.

Gibbs uses for his definition a cell system Ω^γ in the γ-space, based upon Boltzmann's cell system Ω^μ in the μ-space. Ω^μ was a division of the total range R^μ into K μ-cells, each having the μ-volume $v^\mu = \dfrac{V^\mu}{K}$. This determines the system Ω^γ, which divides R^γ into $Z = K^N$ γ-cells Q^γ of equal γ-volume $v^\gamma = (v^\mu)^N = \dfrac{(V^\mu)^N}{K^N} = \dfrac{V}{Z}$. A D_i^{ind} determines for each of the N molecules its μ-cell; therefore its range in the γ-space is one γ-cell Q_i^γ. Let D_i^{st} have the μ-cell numbers $N_1, \ldots, N_k$. Then the number of the D^{ind} corresponding to D_i^{st} is $z(D_i^{st}) = \dfrac{N!}{N_1! \ldots N_k!}$. The range of D_i^{st} in the γ-space consists of the z γ-cells representing those D^{ind}.

If any density function $\rho_i(U)$ is given, e.g., determined by a description D_i, then, on the basis of this "fine-grained" density $\rho_i(U)$, the corresponding "*coarse-grained*" density $P_i(U)$ at any point U is defined as the mean of ρ_i over the γ-cell to which U belongs:

For any point U_j within a γ-cell Q_k^γ,

(8-1) $$P_i(U_j) =_{\text{Df}} \frac{1}{v^\gamma} \int_{Q_k^\gamma} \rho_i(U)\, dU$$

Note that P_i, in distinction to ρ_i, is dependent on the cell system Ω^γ. Since P_i has the same value for all points in any given γ-cell, we may regard it as a function of the cells: $P_i(Q_k^\gamma)$.

Let D_j^{ind} have the range Q_j^γ; then we see from (7-12):

(8-2) $$\text{pr}(D_j^{\text{ind}} \mid D_i) = P_i(Q_j^\gamma) v^\gamma.$$

Corresponding to Boltzmann's H-function, Gibbs defines a certain function as an ensemble mean; we denote it by H_G^{II} (because it implicitly uses Method II as we shall see):

(8-3) $$H_G^{\text{II}}(D_i) =_{\text{Df}} \sum_n [P_i(Q_n^\gamma) \ln P_i(Q_n^\gamma)] v^\gamma,$$

where the sum runs through all γ-cells. Hence with (8-1), since $\ln P_i(U)$ has the same value for all points in a cell:

(8-4) $$H_G^{\text{II}}(D_i) = \int_{R^\gamma} \rho_i(U) \ln P_i(U)\, dU.$$

Thus H_G^{II} is the ensemble mean of $\ln P_i$ (see (7-4)), not that of H! [Therefore the notation $\bar{H}$ sometimes used for H_G^{II} is quite misleading; it obviously violates the convention (7-4) concerning the symbol of the mean.]

Gibbs's entropy concept, which we shall denote by 'S_G^{II},' is then defined in analogy to (4-6):

(8-5) $$S_G^{\text{II}}(D_i) =_{\text{Df}} -kH_G^{\text{II}}(D_i).$$

[Actually Gibbs used the term 'temperature' not for T but for $\theta = kT$, and consequently the term 'entropy' not for S_{th} but for S_{th}/k and therefore took as its statistical counterpart not S_G^{II} but S_G^{II}/k. Since the difference is inessential, we explain Gibbs's method by translating it into the more customary terminology.]

We shall now examine Gibbs's concepts H_G^{II} and S_G^{II}. They are, like Boltzmann's concepts H and S_B, dependent upon the choice of a cell system, but, in distinction to Boltzmann's original concepts, they have the advantage that they are not restricted to D^{st} but applicable to any form of description with any region in the γ-space as its range.

Let D_i be a disjunction of $m\, D^{ind}$ (not necessarily corresponding to the same D^{st}). Let these D^{ind} be represented by the m γ-cells $Q_1, \ldots, Q_m$. Then the range $R(D_i)$ consists of these m γ-cells and thus has the volume mv^γ. Therefore the density ρ_i based on D_i has for every point of this range the value $1/(mv^\gamma)$ (see (7-11)). Thus this is likewise the value of P_i for each of the m γ-cells. Hence from (8-3):

(8-6) $\qquad\qquad H^{II}_G(D_i) = -\ln(mv^\gamma).$

(8-7) $\qquad\qquad S^{II}_G(D_i) = k(\ln m + \ln v^\gamma).$

Hence with (6-11) (b):

(8-8) $\qquad\qquad S^{II}_G(D_i) = S^{II}_B(D_i) + kN \ln N.$

Thus $S^{II}_G(D_i)$ is, aside from an additive constant, the same as $S^{II}_B(D_i)$. Therefore S^{II}_G possesses likewise the essential features of Method II.

We shall now examine some special cases of descriptions of the specified form D_i.

Case 1. Let D_i be a D^{st}_i; then $m = z(D^{st}_i)$.

Hence:

(8-9) $\qquad\qquad H^{II}_G(D^{st}_i) = -(\ln z(D^{st}_i) + \ln v^\gamma).$

(8-10) $\qquad\qquad S^{II}_G(D^{st}_i) = k(\ln z(D^{st}_i) + \ln v^\gamma).$

For a fixed, sufficiently large N and a fixed cell system, these values differ from those of H and S_B, respectively, only by an additive constant (see (4-5) and (4-7)). Thus in the case of a D^{st}, Gibbs's concept of entropy is like Boltzmann's, in agreement with S_{th} under the conditions previously mentioned (§5). However, we shall see that this agreement holds only for D^{st}.

Case 2. Let D_i be a D^{ind}; then $m = 1$ and hence:

(8-11) $\qquad\qquad H^{II}_G(D^{ind}_i) = -\ln v^\gamma.$

(8-12) $\qquad\qquad S^{II}_G(D^{ind}_i) = k \ln v^\gamma.$

Thus S^{II}_G has the same value for all D^{ind}, irrespective of the physical properties of the state of the gas as described in the D^{ind}.

EXAMINATION OF THE STATISTICAL CONCEPT OF ENTROPY 53

As a consequence of the use of Method II, S_G^{II} like S_B^{II} has in this case no relation to S_{th}; moreover, it is not a physical concept but a purely logical one.

Case 3. Let D_i be a disjunction D_1 of p_1 D^{st} such that in any two of these D^{st} the cell numbers N_j for any μ-cell Q_j are either equal or nearly equal. Then all these D^{st} have practically the same value of z, say z_1, and therefore also of S_B, say $S_{B,1}$, and of S_G^{II} (8-10), say $S_{G,1}^{II} = k(\ln z_1 + \ln v^\gamma)$. Suppose that the conditions for agreement between S_B and S_{th} stated in §5 are satisfied; the p_1 D^{st} may, for example, be those which are compatible as typical D^{st} for an interval around t_1 with some measurements of temperature and pressure made at various places in the gas. More specifically, let us take the model explained at the end of §5; the vessel is divided by walls perforated by small holes. At any time during the process, the gas g is in each part of the vessel in a state of near-equilibrium. We have $m = m_1 = p_1 z_1$, and hence with (8-7): $S_G^{II}(D_1) = k[\ln (p_1 z_1) + \ln v^\gamma] = S_{G,1}^{II} + k \ln p_1$. Suppose that an interval around t_2 is only a short time later than the first and still within the period of equalization. Suppose that in this interval similar measurements are made, with slightly different results but much greater precision. Let D_2 be again the disjunction of the corresponding D^{st}; let their number be p_2. Let z_2, $S_{B,2}$, and $S_{G,2}^{II}$ be the values which hold (practically) for each of these D^{st}. Then: $S_G^{II}(D_2) = k[\ln (p_2 z_2) + \ln v^\gamma]$. Because of the equalization, we have $S_{th}(g, t_2) > S_{th}(g, t_1)$; therefore $S_{B,2} > S_{B,1}$, $S_{G,2}^{II} > S_{G,1}^{II}$, and $z_2 > z_1$. We assume that the holes are very small and therefore the rate of equalization very low and that $t_2 - t_1$ is small. Therefore the increase in z will be small. On the other hand, we assume that the precision of the measurements at t_2 is much greater than that at t_1 and therefore p_2 is much smaller than p_1, so much smaller that $m_2 = p_2 z_2 < m_1 = p_1 z_1$. Hence:

(8-13) $$S_G^{II}(D_2) < S_G^{II}(D_1).$$

Thus for the descriptions D_1 and D_2 of the kind described, which are (practically) typical descriptions of g for t_1 and t_2 respectively, we find a decrease in S_G^{II} in spite of an increase in S_{th}. This shows that in cases of this kind Gibbs's concept S_G^{II} is not in accord with S_{th}.

Case 4. The application of S_G^{II} to the description D_1^S in Example 4 in §6 would lead to a result which is analogous to (6-25) and just as strange.

Thus we are led to the conclusion that Gibbs did not reach his aim of constructing a statistical concept corresponding to S_{th}. The correspondence holds for his concept only in the special case of D^{st}. And in Gibbs's method the concept cannot be restricted to D^{st}; this will be seen in the discussion of his H-theorem.

Gibbs has stated for his function H_G^{II} a theorem which is regarded as an analogue to Boltzmann's H-theorem (5-2):

(8-14) *Gibbs's "generalized H-theorem"* for his function H_G^{II}. Let D_1 be set up as a typical description for g on the basis of measurements made during a time interval around t_1, with given N and the total energy lying in a small interval around E. Then H_G^{II} will diminish and hence S_G^{II} increase in the course of time until the representative ensemble is nearly evenly spread out over the γ-cells of the given E-interval.

Various arguments have been proposed to prove this theorem or to make it at least plausible on the basis of various additional assumptions (see, e.g., Tolman, op. cit., pp. 169–179).

We shall give here a simple proof of a partial assertion of (8-14) which gives a comparison between the states at t_1 and some later time t_2. Our main purpose is to clarify the physical meaning of the decrease in H_G^{II}.

Let D_1 be a disjunction of m_1 D^{ind} which have the same or nearly the same μ-cell numbers N_j, typical for the gas g during an interval around t_1. If D_1 is based on measurements, it may, for example, be a D^{st}, as in Case 1 discussed above (with $m_1 = z_1$), or a disjunction of p_1 D^{st} as in Case 3 (with $m_1 = p_1 z_1$); however, this is not necessary for the following proof. Let D_2 be that description of g at t_2 which is derived from D_1 under the assumption of constant energy (see the explanation at the end of §7). Let R_1 be the range of D_1 in the γ-space, and R_2 that of D_2. R_1 consists of m_1 γ-cells; therefore its volume is $v_1 = m_1 v^\gamma$. The density ρ_1 for D_1 is $1/(m_1 v^\gamma)$ within R_1 and 0 outside. According to Liouville's theorem ((7-15) and (7-16)), the volume v_2 of R_2 is likewise $m_1 v^\gamma$, and the density ρ_2 for D_2 is $1/(m_1 v^\gamma)$ within R_2 and 0 outside. Suppose that R_2 extends into m_2 cells, $Q_{2,n}^\gamma (n=1,\ldots,m_2)$, and that the volume of the part of $Q_{2,n}^\gamma$ covered by R_2 is $q_n v^\gamma$. Hence for every $n(=1,\ldots,m_2)$, $0 < q_n \leq 1$. Since $v_2 = m_1 v^\gamma$:

$$(8\text{-}15) \qquad \sum_{n=1}^{m_2} q_n = m_1.$$

Since the ensemble changes its shape all the time, it seems quite plausible to assume that at t_2, although its volume is still $m_1 v^\gamma$, it does not exactly consist of entire cells only; in other words, that at least one of the cells $Q_{2,n}^\gamma$ is not completely covered by it:

(8-16) Assumption.
  (a) For at least one n, $0 < q_n < 1$; hence
  (b) $m_2 > m_1$.

Let P_2 be the coarse-grained density for D_2; then from (8-1):

(8-17) For $n = 1, \ldots, m_2$, $P_2(Q_{2,n}) = \dfrac{1}{v^\gamma} \dfrac{q_n v^\gamma}{m_1 v^\gamma} = \dfrac{q_n}{m_1 v^\gamma}$; for all other cells, $P_2 = 0$.

Therefore with (8-3) and (8-15):

(8-18) $$H_G^{II}(D_2) = \sum_{n=1}^{m_2} \left[\dfrac{q_n}{m_1 v^\gamma} \ln \dfrac{q_n}{m_1 v^\gamma} \right] v^\gamma$$
$$= \dfrac{1}{m_1} \sum [q_n \ln q_n] - \ln(m_1 v^\gamma).$$

From (8-16):

(8-19) $$H_G^{II}(D_1) = -\ln(m_1 v^\gamma).$$

(8-20) (a) $H_G^{II}(D_1) - H_G^{II}(D_2) = -\dfrac{1}{m_1} \sum_{n=1}^{m_2} [q_n \ln q_n],$
  (b) $\phantom{H_G^{II}(D_1) - H_G^{II}(D_2) =}\,> 0$. (From (8-16) (a).)

Thus H_G^{II} decreases from t_1 to t_2.

Gibbs's theorem is supposed to be, like Boltzmann's H-theorem, a statistical counterpart to the second law of thermodynamics. However, there are striking differences between Gibbs's and Boltzmann's theorems in two points. First, at least the partial assertion (8-20) (b) does not, like Boltzmann's theorem, involve probability; it states that H_G^{II} decreases and S_G^{II} increases from t_1 to t_2 *with certainty*, once the assumption (8-16) (a) is granted. And we see from (8-20) (a) that the amount by which H_G^{II} decreases depends merely upon the number m_2 of cells and the fractions q_n of these cells covered by R_2; the amount is independent of the physical properties of these cells and, in particular, of the values of H and of S_{th} for the gas states represented by these cells.

Thus the decrease in H_G^{II} has nothing whatever to do with a decrease in H and an increase in S_{th}. Therefore *Gibbs's theorem is not a generalization of Boltzmann's H-theorem, and has nothing to do with the second law of thermodynamics.* This will become still clearer by the consideration of two special cases.

Case 5. Suppose that g is in a state of local near-equilibrium both at t_1 and at t_2. Let $S_B(t_1)$ be the mean S_B for an interval around t_1 and $S_B(t_2)$ the mean S_B for a very short interval around t_2. Suppose that $S_B(t_2)$ is smaller than $S_B(t_1)$ by a very small amount, but that this amount and the second interval are still large enough for measurement. According to the statistical conception, this case is not impossible although its probability is extremely small, so that for all practical purposes we may disregard the case. We consider now this case, not for practical purposes, but only in order to clarify the meaning of S_G^{II}. In this exceptional case, the mean S_B and therefore the measurable S_{th} decrease, but according to (8-20) (b), S_G^{II} nevertheless increases. This shows again that S_G^{II} has nothing to do with S_{th}. In this case most of the new cells into which the ensemble has spread by t_2 represent states with lower values of S_B and of S_{th}. S_G^{II} in no way reflects this fact; it merely reflects the fact of spreading.

Case 6. Let D_1 be a typical D^{st} with the minimum value of H for the given E, and therefore the maximum of S_B and of S_{th}. Thus g is at t_1 in a state of (total, not only local) statistical and thermodynamic equilibrium. While Boltzmann's theorem contains the condition that $H(D_1^{st})$ be above the mean and thus does not apply to the present case, Gibbs's theorem is not restricted in this respect. Obviously, in this case, S_B cannot possibly increase and will most probably even decrease (by a very small amount); and S_{th} cannot increase. Even Gibbs's own function S_G^{II} has in this case for D_1 the maximum value among all D^{st} for the given E. (See the remark on (8-10) above). Nevertheless, according to (8-20) (b), S_G^{II} is higher for D_2 than for D_1 (this is possible only because D_2 is not a D^{st}). It may even be considerably higher, and thus the discrepancy between S_G^{II} and S_{th} may be considerable. [This is seen as follows. H_G^{II} has its minimum in the given E-interval if m_2 is the number m_E of cells for the E-interval and all q_n are equal and hence, with (8-15), $= m_1/m_E$. If $H_G^{II}(D_2)$ has this minimum value, $H_G^{II}(D_1) - H_G^{II}(D_2)$ is, according to (8-20) (a), $= \ln(m_E/m_1)$. Although those D^{st} whose S_B is equal or near the maximum S_B for the E-interval have *together* a high probability and cover a majority of the m_E cells, nevertheless, since the number of these D^{st} is large, our D_1 alone, which is one of them, covers only a small part of the cells. Therefore m_1/m_E is a small fraction.]

A short remark only about the development of the ensemble after the time t_2: Suppose that at a later time t_3 the ensemble has spread into m_3 cells with q-values $q_{n'}$ ($n' = 1, \ldots, m_3$). Then a sufficient and necessary condition for H_G^{II} being smaller at t_3 than at t_2 is that $\sum_{n=1}^{m_2} \left(q_n \ln \frac{1}{q_n}\right) < \sum_{n=1}^{m_3} \left(q_{n'} \ln \frac{1}{q_{n'}}\right)$; hence that there is an increase from t_2 to t_3 in the degree of disorder of the distribution of the ensemble points over the γ-cells. This condition means roughly a spreading into still more cells and a more even distribution of the q-values. It does *not* mean an increase in the degree of disorder of the distribution of the phase points of the molecules among the μ-cells, which would be equivalent to an increase in S_B. Thus the logical situation with Gibbs's theorem is as follows. By an analysis of the laws of mechanics (similar to the analysis which led to Liouville's theorem) the physicists regard it as plausible that the following assumption holds with very great probability (i.e., in the great majority of all possible cases)!

(A) If at t_1 the degree of disorder of the distribution of a given ensemble among the γ-cells is not near to its maximum (which is the state in which the ensemble covers an equal fraction q of every γ-cell corresponding to the given E), then at a later time t_2 the degree of disorder will be higher than at t_1.

From (A) the following can be inferred:

(B) If at t_1 H_G^{II} for a given ensemble is not near to its minimum value for the given E, then at a later time t_2 H_G^{II} will be lower. (B) is essentially Gibbs's theorem. (B) is mathematically deducible from (A). Now our discussions have shown that from the mere statement of the decrease of H_G^{II} in (B) nothing can be inferred about a change in S_B or in S_{th}.

9
An Alternative Definition of Entropy for an Ensemble.

Summary. We define H_G^I as the ensemble mean of H^I and S_G^I as $-kH_G^I$. Then S_G^I is the ensemble mean of our S_B^I (§6). We propose S_G^I as an alternative to Gibbs's S_G^{II}. In contrast to the latter, S_G^I is in agreement with S_{th} not only for D^{st} but also for more specific or less specific descriptions. A generalized H-theorem (9-12) involving our concepts H_G^I and S_G^I is formulated, which follows from the same assumptions as Boltzmann's H-theorem. This theorem is, in contrast to Gibbs's theorem (8-14), a statistical counterpart to the second law of thermodynamics.

We shall now construct an alternative concept which, in distinction to Gibbs's S_G^{II}, fulfills the following conditions: (1) it satisfies the principles (6-1) and (6-2) and is therefore a purely physical concept; (2) it is in agreement with S_{th} or with the mean of S_{th} in an ensemble (under the same conditions as S_B, §5); (3) it leads to a theorem which is an analogue to Boltzmann's H-theorem and a statistical counterpart to the second law. The property (1) is assured by the use of Method I (§6); we therefore denote the concept by 'S_G^I'. Although it is not Gibbs's concept, we retain the subscript 'G', because we follow Gibbs in applying the concept to a representative ensemble in the γ-space.

In §6 we defined H^I for a D_i^{prec} as an extension of Boltzmann's H is accordance with Method I, with respect to a given cell-system (6-9). We assign now the same value of H^I to the phase point U_i which represents D_i^{prec} in the γ-space:

(9-1) $H^I(U_i) =_{Df} H(D_i^{st})$, where D_i^{st} is that D^{st} to whose range in the γ-space the point U_i belongs.

Hence from (4-4) (a):

(9-2) $H^I(U_i) = \sum (N_j \ln N_j) - \ln v^\gamma$, where the N_j ($j = 1, \ldots, K$) are the μ-cell numbers of D_i^{st}.

Now we define H_G^I for any description D_i as the ensemble mean of $H^I(U)$, in accordance with (7-4):

(9-3) $H_G^I(D_i) =_{Df} \int H^I(U) \, \rho_i(U) \, dU$, where ρ_i is the density function determined by D_i.

EXAMINATION OF THE STATISTICAL CONCEPT OF ENTROPY

Since the aim is to construct an analogue to Boltzmann's H-function, it seems more natural to take the mean of H^1 than that of $\ln P_i$, as Gibbs does. [The notation $\bar{H}$, which is sometimes used for Gibbs's H_G^{II}, could correctly be applied to our concept; or, more specifically, the notation '$\bar{H}^1$'.] For all points U of a γ-cell Q_n^γ, $H^1(U)$ has the same value $H^1(Q_n^\gamma)$; therefore:

$$(9\text{-}4) \qquad H_G^1(D_i) = \sum_n [H^1(Q_n^\gamma) P_i(Q_n^\gamma)] v^\gamma,$$

where $\sum$ extends over all γ-cells.

Now we define our entropy concept in analogy to (8-5):

$$(9\text{-}5) \qquad S_G^1(D_i) =_{Df} -k H_G^1(D_i).$$

Thus S_G^1 is the ensemble mean of S_B^1, which is our extension (6-4) of Boltzmann's S_B.

Let D_i be a disjunction of m descriptions $D_n^{ind}(n = 1, \ldots, m)$. We found earlier (§8) that, for each of the m γ-cells Q_n^γ in the range of D_i, $P_i = 1/(mv^\gamma)$ and otherwise $P_i = 0$. Hence with (9-4):

$$(9\text{-}6) \qquad H_G^1(D_i) = \frac{1}{m} \sum_{n=1}^{m} H^1(Q_n^\gamma).$$

$$(9\text{-}7) \qquad S_G^1(D_i) = -\frac{k}{m} \sum_{n=1}^{m} H^1(Q_n^\gamma) = \frac{1}{m} \sum_{n=1}^{m} S_B^1(D_n^{ind}).$$

Thus $S_G^1(D_i)$ is the mean of S_B^1 for the disjunctive components in D_i.

In order to compare our concepts with those of Gibbs, let us examine the results for the Cases 1 to 4 in §8.

Case 1. Let D_i be a D_i^{st}. Then from (6-5) and (6-6):

$$(9\text{-}8) \qquad H_G^1(D_i^{st}) = H(D_i^{st}),$$

and

$$(9\text{-}9) \qquad S_G^1(D_i^{st}) = S_B(D_i^{st}).$$

Thus in the case of a D^{st}, our S_G^1 coincides exactly with Boltzmann's S_B. We saw that S_G^{II} does essentially the same (approximately, and with another additive constant; these differences may be regarded as inessential).

Case 2. Let D_i be a D^{ind}; hence $m = 1$. Let D_i^{ind} be represented by the cell Q_i^γ. Then:

(9-10) $H_G^I(D_i^{ind}) = H^I(Q_i^\gamma)$.

(9-11) $S_G^I(D_i^{ind}) = S_B^I(D_i^{ind}) = S_B(D_i^{st})$, where D_i^{st} is the D^{st} corresponding to D_i^{ind}.

Thus for a D^{ind}, S_G^I coincides with our extension S_B^I of S_B, and with the value of S_B for the corresponding D^{st}. Since Boltzmann's $S_B(D_i^{st})$ and our S_B^I (D_i^{ind}) are in agreement with S_{th} (under the conditions stated in §5), the same holds for $S_G^I(D_i^{st})$ and $S_G^I(D_i^{ind})$. We found that S_G^{II} in this case has no relation to S_{th}.

Case 3. Let D_i be a disjunction D_1 of p_1 D^{st} with nearly equal N_j. These D^{st} are assumed to be compatible with measurements made at t_1. Similarly, let D_2 be a disjunction of p_2 D^{st}, related to measurements of much greater precision at t_2. It was assumed that p_2 was much smaller than p_1 so that even $p_2 z_2 < p_1 z_1$, although $z_2 > z_1$. However, in distinction to S_G^{II}, the value of $S_G^I(D_1)$ is independent of p_1; it is $= S_{G,1}^I$, i.e., $S_G^I(D_1^{st})$, where D_1^{st} is any of the D^{st} in D_1; hence $= S_{B,1}$, i.e. $S_B(D_1^{st})$; hence $= S_{th}(g, t_1)$. Similarly, $S_G^I(D_2) = S_B(D_2^{st}) = S_{th}(g, t_2)$. Thus S_G^I is at both times in agreement with S_{th} and increases from t_1 to t_2 just like S_{th}. In contrast, we found that, due to the influence of the numbers p_1 and p_2 (which are characteristic of the precision of the measurements at t_1 and t_2, respectively, but have nothing to do with the values obtained by the measurements) $S_G^{II}(D_2) < S_G^{II}(D_1)$ (8-13); thus the change in S_G^{II} is in the opposite direction to that in S_{th}.

Case 4. Let D_i be the description D_1^S in Example 4 in §6. D_1^S says that the mean S_B for the given period of time is near to -10^7 k. We see from (9-7) that $S_G^I(D_1^S) = -10^7$ k, which is, just like S_B, in agreement with S_{th}. In contrast, Gibbs' concept leads to the paradoxical result $S_G^{II}(D_1^S) = -13.8$ k, a glaring divergence from S_{th}.

Thus the result of the comparison between S_G^I and S_G^{II} is as follows. In the case of a D^{st} both concepts are in agreement with S_{th} (under the conditions of equilibrium and typical description). However, for any description which is either more specific than a D^{st}, e.g., a D^{ind}, or less specific, e.g., a disjunction of several D^{st} with equal or nearly equal S_B, S_G^I is still in agreement with S_{th}, while S_G^{II} deviates from S_{th}, sometimes by a very large amount.

We shall now formulate an analogue to Boltzmann's H-theorem (5-2) for our function H_G^1 and consider the question of its validity. Let D_1^{st} be a typical description of an isolated gas body g at the time t_1 with total energy E; let D_2 and D_3 be derived from D_1^{st} according to the laws of mechanics (§7) for the later time points t_2 and t_3, respectively ($t_1 < t_2 < t_3$). Let $\bar{H}_E$ be the mean value of $H(D^{st})$ for the given E. $[\bar{H}_E = \sum_{i=1}^{m}[H(D_i^{st})z(D_i^{st})]/\sum_{i=1}^{m}z(D_i^{st})$. In virtue of (4-9), where m is the number of D^{st} for the given E.]

(9-12) *Generalized H-theorem for H_G^1.* The following relations hold with overwhelming probability:
(a) If $H(D_1^{st})$ is considerably higher than $\bar{H}_E$, $H_G^1(D_1^{st}) > H_G^1(D_2)$ and therefore $S_G^1(D_1^{st}) < S_G^1(D_2)$.
(b) If $H_G^1(D_2)$ is considerably higher than $\bar{H}_E$, $H_G^1(D_2) > H_G^1(D_3)$ and therefore $S_G^1(D_2) < S_G^1(D_3)$.

We shall now show, that, if the assumptions underlying Boltzmann's theorem are valid (we do not decide whether they are or not), then (9-12) is valid. Let R_1 be the range of D_1^{st} in the γ-space, R_2 that of D_2, and R_3 that of D_3. Let $D_{1,i}^{prec}$ (with variable i) be any one of those D^{prec} which correspond to D_1^{st}. Let $D_{2,i}^{prec}$ and $D_{3,i}^{prec}$ be derived from $D_{1,i}^{prec}$ for t_2 and t_3, respectively. Let $D_{2,i}^{st}$ and $D_{3,i}^{st}$ be the S^{st} corresponding to $D_{2,i}^{prec}$ and $D_{3,i}^{prec}$, respectively. Let $U_{1,i}$, $U_{2,i}$, and $U_{3,i}$ be the phase points of $D_{1,i}^{prec}$, $D_{2,i}^{prec}$ and $D_{3,i}^{prec}$, respectively. ($U_{1,i}$ runs through R_1, $U_{2,i}$ through R_2, and $U_{3,i}$ through R_3.) From (9-1):

(i) $\qquad H^I(U_{1,i}) = H(D_1^{st})$, $H^I(U_{2,i}) = H(D_{2,i}^{st})$, and
$\qquad H^I(U_{3,i}) = H(D_{3,i}^{st})$.

Boltzmann's theorem says in effect that the following relations hold with great probability if the conditions about $\bar{H}_E$ in (9-12) (a) and (b) are fulfilled:

(ii) $\qquad H(D_{1,i}^{st}) > H(D_{2,i}^{st})$ and $H(D_{2,i}^{st}) > H(D_{3,i}^{st})$;

hence with (i):

(iii) $\qquad H^I(U_{1,i}) > H^I(U_{2,i})$ and $H^I(U_{2,i}) > H^I(U_{3,i})$.

As earlier stated (§5), the reasoning leading to Boltzmann's theorem is not a rigorous proof; it rather shows that, if certain highly plausible assumptions are made, the relation asserted in this theorem holds in the average over a great number of possible cases. Thus the result of the reasoning can be formulated, more appropriately than by (ii), by saying that (iii) holds in the average for the ensemble in question. [This is explained, e.g., by Tolman, op. cit., pp. 146 f.] Now H_G^1 was defined in (9-3) as the ensemble mean of $H^1(U)$. Therefore:

(iv) $H_G^1(D_1^{st})$ is the ensemble mean of $H^1(U_{1,i})$,

(v) $H_G^1(D_2)$ is the ensemble mean of $H^1(U_{2,i})$,

(vi) $H_G^1(D_3)$ is the ensemble mean of $H^1(U_{3,i})$.

Thus the more appropriate formulation is as follows:
(vii) With great probability, (a) $H_G^1(D_1^{st}) > H_G^1(D_2)$, and
(vii) (b) $H_G^1(D_2) > H_G^1(D_3)$.
This is the theorem (9-12).

[Although we do not analyze in detail the reasoning leading to Boltzmann's theorem, some remarks may be made to indicate the weakest point in this reasoning. (Tolman, op. cit., pp. 148–152, discusses essentially the same point in greater detail and emphasizes the lack of proof for the assumptions involved. Unfortunately, his explanations and formulas there and at many other places throughout his chapter on H are not quite clear and are sometimes even ambiguous because he speaks of H "for a system s at time t" without explicitly specifying the description of s at t for which H is meant and without indicating how H is defined for other than statistical descriptions.) This point concerns part (b) of (9-12). At first glance, (b) may appear as perfectly analogous to and deducible from (a). But this is not the case, because D_1^{st} is a D^{st}, while D_2 is not. Let D_2' be the disjunction of all D^{st} whose ranges overlap with R_2, among them $D_{2,i}^{st}$. Hence the range R_2' of D_2' includes R_2. Let D_3' be derived from D_2' for t_3. Hence the range R_3' of D_3' includes R_3. Let $(D_{2,i}^{st})_3$ be derived from $D_{2,i}^{st}$ for t_3. Then (a), although not applicable to D_2, can be applied to each D^{st} in D_2', e.g., $D_{2,i}^{st}$. Let us assume that (9-12) (a) is valid. Then:

(viii) If $H(D_{2,i}^{st})$ is considerably higher than $\bar{H}_E$,

$$H_G^1(D_{2,i}^{st}) > H_G^1(D_{2,i}^{st})_3,$$

and analogously for every other D^{st} in D_2'. Therefore, an analogous relation holds for the means:

(ix) If $H_G^l(D_2')$ is considerably higher than $\bar{H}_E$,

$$H_G^l(D_2') > H_G^l(D_3').$$

This is not yet (b). It refers to D_2' and D_3', while (b) refers to D_2 and D_3. But we can infer (b) from (ix) and hence from (a) if we make the following assumption:

(x) With great probability, H_G^l has approximately equal values for D_2 and D_2', and likewise for D_3 and D_3'.

This assumption can be made plausible by considering that H_G^l is the ensemble mean of $H^l(U)$ and the latter is constant within the range of any D^{st} and changes only very little from any such range to an adjacent one. However, the plausibility of (x) is weaker than that of the assumptions needed for part (a).

The assumptions needed for theorem (9-12) are the same as those needed for Boltzmann's theorem. Their necessity for the latter was discovered by Gibbs and his followers when they tried to reformulate Boltzmann's theorem and the reasoning leading to it in Gibbs's language. The refinement consisted chiefly in replacing Boltzmann's references to the values of certain magnitudes for a single physical system by references to the ensemble means of these magnitudes. Our theorem (9-12) has thus the same status as Boltzmann's. It might indeed be regarded as merely a practically equivalent formulation of the latter in Gibbs's ensemble language.

Let us assume that, at any moment during the whole time considered, g fulfills the condition of local near-equilibrium stated earlier (§5). Then S_B^l is in accord with S_{th}. S_G^l is the ensemble mean of S_B^l and thus is, in contrast to S_G^{ll}, in accord with the average of S_{th} for the ensemble. Therefore, theorem (9-12) is, like Boltzmann's, but in contrast to Gibbs's theorem (8-14), *a statistical counterpart to the second law of thermodynamics.*

10
Entropy and Amount of Information

Summary. Let inf be the amount of information (either in the statistical sense (10-1) or in the semantical sense (10-4), which have the same value under certain conditions). For any D^{st}, $S^* = -\text{inf}$ (10-12); a similar relation holds between S_B and inf (10-13). It is sometimes said that this relation holds generally, for all kinds of descriptions. However, this is the case only for those extended concepts which are formed by Method II, viz., S_B^{II} (6-11) and S^{*II} (10-15). We saw earlier (§6) that a concept of this kind is not a physical but a logical concept; now we see just which logical property it measures, viz. the negative amount of information. The general statement does not hold for the concepts formed by Method I. Szilard solved the paradox of Maxwell's demon by pointing out that the demon, in order to measure the velocity of an approaching molecule, must dissipate some energy and thereby increase the entropy. This is correct, but the conclusion drawn by later authors that in this process negative entropy is transformed into information and vice versa seems rather questionable.

In the mathematical theory of communication,[1] it is customary to define the amount of information in the following way. A finite set of messages or statements D_i is given, with probabilities pr (D_i) assigned to them. We shall use here the term 'statistical information' and the symbol 'inf$_{stat}$' in order to distinguish this concept from another one to be introduced soon. The definition is as follows ('Log' denotes the logarithm to base 2):

(10-1) $\quad \text{inf}_{stat}(D_i) =_{Df} -\text{Log pr}(D_i) = \text{Log} \dfrac{1}{\text{pr}(D_i)}.$

In order to apply this concept, we make use of Boltzmann's probability assumption (4-8):

(10-2) $\quad$ For every D_i^{ind}, $\text{inf}_{stat} D_i^{ind} = \text{Log } Z = N \text{ Log } K.$

Strictly speaking, this and the other values of inf stated further on refer to the amount of information relative to some prior knowledge represented by a description D_0 of the physical system in question, say the gas g. Throughout the following discussion on information we regard D_0 as given. D_0 states the value of N, the total range R^μ

---

[1] Claude E. Shannon and Warren Weaver, *The Mathematical Theory of Communication* (Urbana: University of Illinois Press, 1949).

in the μ-space and a cell system Ω^μ with K cells. Thus we can infer from D_0 the volume V^μ of R^μ and the cell volume v^μ; furthermore, in the γ-space, the total range R^γ and its volume V^γ, the cell system Ω^γ and the cell volume v^γ. [Note that D_0 does not state the energy E, and that (10-2) refers to the totality of all D^{ind} for the given N and K, not only to those of a given energy level.]

Together with Y. Bar-Hillel, I have developed a semantical theory of information.[2] In distinction to the statistical theory mentioned above, it takes into consideration the meaning or content of the statements. We have defined several concepts to explicate the amount of information. These concepts are, in our opinion, closer than the statistical concept to the meaning intended by scientists in pre-systematic talk when they say that one statement is stronger in content or carries more information than another. While the statistical concept of information is based on the statistical concept of probability (which means relative frequency in the long run), our theory uses a logical or inductive concept of probability. For our present discussion, we shall use that function m_D of initial probability (see §2) which has equal values for all state-descriptions, that is, in the present context, for all D^{ind}:

(10-3) $\qquad$ For every D_i^{ind}, $m_D(D_i^{ind}) = \dfrac{1}{Z}$.

Then we define the *amount of semantical information*:

(10-4) $\quad$ For any statement D_i, $\inf_{sem}(D_i) =_{Df} -\text{Log } m_D(D_i)$.

Hence:

(10-5) $\quad$ For every D_i^{ind}, $\inf_{sem}(D_i^{ind}) = \text{Log } Z = N \text{ Log } K$.

(In our treatise of 1952, the function $\inf_{sem}$ based on m_D is denoted by '$\inf_D$.')

We see from (10-2) and (10-5) that, under the assumptions made here, the functions $\inf_{stat}$ and $\inf_{sem}$ agree in their basic values and hence also in their derivative values. Therefore we shall write

---

[2] R. Carnap and Y. Bar-Hillel, *An outline of the theory of semantic information*, Res. Lab. of Electronics, M.I.T. Report No. 247, 1952. A short survey is given in: Bar-Hillel and Carnap, "Semantic Information," *Brit. J. Phil. of Science*, 4 (1953), pp. 147–157; this is a paper read by Bar-Hillel at the Symposium on Applications of Communications Theory (London, September 1952), London, 1953, pp. 503–512.

henceforth simply 'inf,' which may be interpreted either way. Thus:

(10-6) For every D_i^{ind}, $\inf(D_i^{ind}) = \text{Log } Z = N \text{ Log } K$.

For a disjunction of m different D^{ind}, both pr and m_D are m/Z. Hence:

(10-7) If D_i is a disjunction of $m\, D^{ind}$, $\inf(D_i) = \text{Log } \dfrac{Z}{m}$.

A D^{st} is a disjunction of $z\, D^{ind}$; therefore:

(10-8) $\inf(D_i^{st}) = \text{Log } \dfrac{Z}{z(D_i^{st})} = N \text{ Log } K - \text{Log } z(D_i^{st})$.

If the recipient of information obtains a description D_j in addition to his prior knowledge represented by D_i, the increase in information is called the relative amount of information of D_j with respect to D_i, denoted by '$\inf(D_j \mid D_i)$':

(10-9) $\inf(D_j \mid D_i) =_{Df} \inf(D_i \cdot D_j) - \inf(D_i)$.

If D_i is logically implied by D_j, the conjunction $D_i \cdot D_j$ is logically equivalent to D_j; therefore in this case:

(10-10) $\inf(D_j \mid D_i) = \inf(D_j) - \inf(D_i)$.

Let D_i^{st} correspond to D_i^{ind}; then D_i^{st} is logically implied by D_i^{ind}. Hence:

(10-11) $\inf(D_i^{ind} \mid D_i^{st}) = \inf(D_i^{ind}) - \inf(D_i^{st}) = \text{Log } z(D_i^{st})$.

From (10-8), (3-23), and (4-7):

(10-12) $S^*(D_i^{st}) = -\inf(D_i^{st})$,

(10-13) $S_B(D_i^{st}) \cong -k \ln 2 \left[\inf(D_i^{st}) - N \text{ Log } \dfrac{V^\mu}{N} \right]$.

The result (10-12) says that for a D^{st} the entropy S^* is equal to the negative of the amount of information. According to (10-13), a similar relation holds for S_B (aside from an additive constant, which could be abolished by changing the zero point of the S_B-scale, and a constant factor, which could be abolished by changing the unit). Or, if the negative of entropy is called '*negentropy*' as suggested by

Brillouin, the negentropy of a D^{st} is equal or proportional to its amount of information.

In view of this result some authors declare that negentropy is always the same as amount of information. Whether this is the case or not depends upon the method used for extending S to other than statistical descriptions. Let D_i be a disjunction of $m\, D^{ind}$ with respect to a given cell system, with N and K fixed. Then $\inf(D_i) = \text{Log}(Z/m)$ (10-7), $= -\text{Log}\, m + N\, \text{Log}\, K$. Hence from (6-11):

$$(10\text{-}14) \qquad S_B^{II}(D_i) = -k \ln 2 \left[\inf(D_i) - N \log \frac{V^\mu}{N} \right].$$

We extended S^* to S^{*I} in (3-31). S^{*II} would be defined in analogy to (6-11) as follows. Let D_i be a disjunction of $m\, D^{ind}$ ($1 \leq m \leq Z$), then:

$$(10\text{-}15) \qquad S^{*II}(D_i) =_{Df} \text{Log}\, \frac{m}{Z}.$$

Hence:

$$(10\text{-}16) \qquad S^{*II}(D_i^{ind}) = -\text{Log}\, Z = -N\, \text{Log}\, K.$$

$$(10\text{-}17) \qquad S^{*II}(D_i^{st}) = \text{Log}\, \frac{z(D_i^{st})}{Z} = S^*(D_i^{st}).$$

With (6-14):

$$(10\text{-}18) \qquad S^{*II}(D_i) = \text{Log}\, \text{pr}_B(D_i).$$

With (10-7):

$$(10\text{-}19) \qquad S^{*II}(D_i) = -\inf(D_i).$$

Thus for the S concepts constructed according to Method II, the results previously found for D^{st} ((10-12) and (10-13)) hold generally for all D_i of the kind described, which includes the D^{st} and the D^{ind} as special cases. The description D_1^S in Example 4 in §6, which states directly the (approximate) value of S_B for g at t_1, is a special case of D_i with $m/Z = 10^{-6}$. Therefore the above results hold for D_1^S too.

We found earlier that, for any disjunction of D^{ind}, Gibbs's concept S_G^{II} has, aside from an additive constant, the same value as S_B^{II} (see (8-8)). Therefore the relation to inf is for S_G^{II} essentially the same as for S_B^{II}. However, the situation is different in the case to which Gibbs's theorem (8-14) refers. In this case, the description D_1 of g at t_2 is a disjunction of D^{ind}, and the description D_2 is derived from D_1 for the later time t_2 with the help of the laws of mechanics. According to Liouville's theorem (7-15), D_1 and D_2 have the same range volume, therefore the same probability and the same amount of information. On the other hand, according to Gibbs's theorem, S_G^{II} is greater for D_2 than for D_1. Thus the above relation between S_G^{II} and inf does not hold in this case (this is possible because D_2 is not a disjunction of D^{ind}). It is sometimes asserted that the increase of S_G^{II} in the course of time is due to the loss of information, since our prediction of the state of g at a future time t, based on the measurements made at t_1, allegedly becomes more and more uncertain with increasing t. But this assertion is clearly erroneous. On the basis of the laws of mechanics, which are deterministic, not statistical laws, D_1 can be derived from D_2 just as well as D_2 from D_1; therefore both are equally strong, there is no decrease in the amount of information.

In order to clarify the situation with respect to Methods II and I, let us consider a series of descriptions D_1 of the following kind (for a given D_0, i.e., fixed N and K). We represent the descriptions of the series by points on a vertical line (see fig. 3). We begin the series with an arbitrary precise description D_1^{prec}; its range in the γ-space consists of one point U_1. Let Q_1^γ be the γ-cell to which U_1 belongs. We take next some descriptions whose ranges include U_1 and are more and more comprehensive subclasses of Q_1^γ, down to that D^{ind} whose range is Q_1^γ itself; let this be D_1^{ind}. Then we proceed to more and more comprehensive disjunctions consisting of D_1^{ind} and other D^{ind} with the same μ-cell numbers, down to the disjunction of all these D^{ind}, which is the corresponding D_1^{st}. Then we take more and more comprehensive disjunctions of D_1^{st} and other D^{st} with the same value of z, say z_1, down to the disjunction of all of them; let this be D_1^z. This corresponds to a point on the z-scale. Next we take a series of more and more comprehensive disjunctions of several D^z with z-values close to z_1. This corresponds to more and more inclusive intervals on the z-scale around z_1. Let this series end with a description stating the greatest interval around z_1 such that the proportion m_1/Z of all D^{ind} whose z-values belong to the interval does not exceed a fixed small fraction, say 10^{-6}. Let S be either S^* or S_B; then S is a monotone increasing function of z. Therefore the last description states not only an approximate value of z but also an approximate value of S; let this description be D_1^S (it is similar to the D_1^S in Example 4 in §6). Let S^I be the extension of S according to Method I. Then the value of S^I remains the same

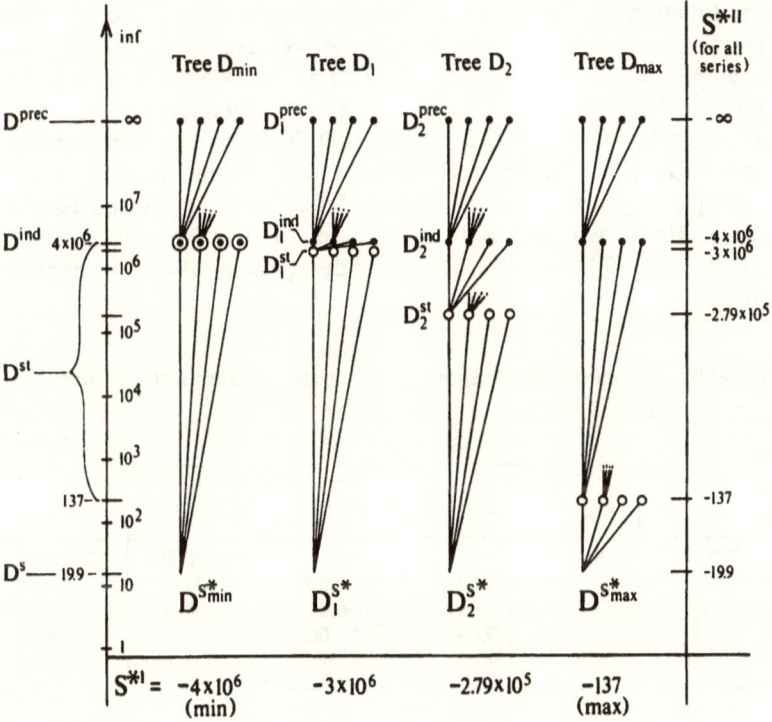

(For the numerical values, see table (10-20).)

Figure 3. Trees of Descriptions.

throughout the series of descriptions from D_1^{prec} to D_1^S (down to D_1^z exactly the same, but further on only approximately, with less and less precision). On the other hand, the probability pr_B increases from 0 to 10^{-6}, and therefore the amount of information inf decreases from ∞ to 19.9. Thus the simple relation of equality between S^I and $-\inf$ (or S^I as a given linear function of inf) which we found for D^{st}, will hold for D_1^{st} but cannot hold for any other description of the series.

Let us illustrate the situation by a *numerical example*. We use the function S^*, for which the simplest relation (10-12) holds. The results for S_B would be analogous. [If we assume, to simplify the example, that $N = V^\mu$, then $S_B(D_i^{st}) = k \ln 2 \times S^*(D_i^{st}) = -k \ln 2 \times \inf(D_i^{st})$.] We take $N = 10^6$, $K = 16$. As μ-cell numbers in the series D_1 we take $N_1 = N_2 = N/2$, all others 0. Then we consider another series D_2 of the same kind, but with the cell numbers as in the example D_{16} at the end of §3 ($N = 99,000$, etc.). In the subsequent *table* (10-20) we refer only to four descriptions from each series: D^{prec}, D^{ind}, D^{st}, and D^{S^*}; the other descriptions have intermediate values.

(10-20) *Numerical example for two series of descriptions with $N = 10^6$, $K = 16$.*

	pr_B	inf	S^{*II} for both series	S^{*I} for D_1	S^{*I} for D_2
D_1^{prec}, D_2^{prec}	0	∞	$-\infty$	$-3,000,000$	$-279,000$
D_1^{ind}, D_2^{ind}	16^{-10^6}	$4,000,000$	$-4,000,000$	$-3,000,000$	$-279,000$
D_1^{st}	8^{-10^6}	$3,000,000$	$-3,000,000$	$-3,000,000$	
D_2^{st}	6.9^{-10^5}	$279,000$	$-279,000$		$-279,000$
$D_1^{S^*} D_2^{S^*}$	10^{-6}	19.9	-19.9	$-3,000,000$	$-279,000$

In the *diagram* (fig. 3), the series D_1 is represented by one of the lines in the tree D_1. And similarly the series D_2 in the tree D_2. The case that all molecules belong to the same μ-cell is represented by the tree D_{min}. In this case, z has its minimum value 1, and hence $S^*(D^{st})$ has its minimum. A D^{st} of this kind coincides with a D^{ind}. The other extreme case is characterized by equal μ-cell numbers; here, z and $S^*(D^{st})$ have their maxima (Tree D_{max}). Two descriptions belonging to different series are represented in the diagram by points on the same horizontal level if they have the same pr_B and therefore the same inf. Thus, all D^{prec} are on the same level;

likewise, all D^{ind} and all D^{S^*}. On the other hand, the D^{st} (represented in the diagram by little circles) are on different levels; the highest possible level of a D^{st} is that in the tree D_{min}, which is the level of the D^{ind} (these D^{st} are represented by circles with dots); the lowest level is that in the tree D_{max}.

Concerning S^{*II} (10-15) and S^{*I} (3-31), the following holds generally for any series of the kind described; for the descriptions of our example we see it from the table. Since S^{*II} is a function of pr_B, it has the same value for descriptions on the same level in different series. (Therefore in the diagram the values are given in a marginal *column*.) Since S^{*II} is equal to $-\inf$ (10-19), it is monotone increasing in each series. In contrast, S^{*I} has the same value throughout each series, but different values for different series with different z. (Therefore, in the diagram, the values are given in a marginal *row*.) This situation makes it clear that S^{*I} is a physical property; as we know, it is a certain function of $\ln z$ which (aside from the unit chosen) is in agreement with thermodynamic entropy S_{th}. On the other hand, S^{*II} cuts across S_{th} and represents merely a logical property, in particular the negative amount of information.

Perhaps the adherents of Method II will reply that S_B^{II} ought not to be regarded as a logical concept, because its various values for D^{st} always coincide with those of the original concept S_B, whose character as a physical concept is not questioned. However, the fact of this coincidence does not prove that S_B^{II} is not a logical concept. For *any* physical magnitude M with a continuous scale, we can in general find a class C^M of descriptions D^M of the following kind: (1) each description D_i^M ascribes to a physical system a value x_i of M with some precision, in other words, a small interval of length Δ_i around x_i; (2) for any one of these descriptions D_i^M, its amount of information is proportional to the value x_i in question: $\inf(D_i^M) = Ax_i$, with a fixed constant A. Suppose that there is a probability density function δ over the scale of M; then the probability that the value of M lies within a small interval of length Δ around x_i is $\Delta \cdot \delta(x_i)$. Now we define the class C^M as follows: it contains those descriptions D_i^M in which, for any x_i, $\Delta_i = 2^{-Ax_i}/\delta(x_i)$. Then $\text{pr}(D_i^M) = 2^{-Ax_i}$; hence, with (10-1), $\inf(D_i^M) = Ax_i$. For $A = -1$, we should have $\inf = -x_i$; this is the case with S^* for the class of the D^{st} (10-12). Thus, there is nothing mysterious about the fact (10-12) that for a certain class of descriptions there is a simple relation between the physical value stated and a certain logical measure of the description.

The main result of our discussions is that *the general statement of equality of entropy and negative amount of information can be* *maintained only if Method II is chosen. However, in this case the resulting concept S^{II} (in any of its versions) is not a physical but a logical concept.* The customary use of the term 'entropy' for this concept is apt to lead to confusion. The simplest way of solving the terminological problem would be to use for S^{II} the term 'negative amount of information'; hence for $-S^{II}$ not 'negentropy' but 'amount of information.'

Although the general identification of entropy (as a physical concept) with the negative amount of information cannot be maintained, there are certainly important relations between these two concepts. So far we have discussed only one relation, the equality or proportionality in the case of D^{st}. Another important relation was first pointed out by *Szilard*.[3] He analyzes the much discussed paradox of *Maxwell's demon*.[4] Suppose that the vessel containing a gas is divided by a wall into two parts A and B with equal temperature. Maxwell imagines a little demon who is able to observe individual molecules of the gas and to operate a door covering a hole in the wall. He opens the door only when a molecule of high velocity in A or one of low velocity in B approaches. Thus, without expenditure of work, the temperature in B is continually increased and that in A decreased, in contradiction to the second law of thermodynamics. Szilard points out that the demon or an automatic apparatus, in order to ascertain the velocity of the approaching molecule a_i, has to make an experiment, say with light rays reflected by a_i. This experiment involved inevitably the dissipation of some energy and hence a corresponding increase in entropy for the total system consisting of the gas, the apparatus, the radiation, etc. This increase in entropy cancels out the decrease brought about by the transfer of a_i to the other part of the vessel. Thus the second law is not violated.

Szilard's idea has been further developed by later authors. In particular *L. Brillouin*, in several articles,[5] has investigated the relation between negentropy and amount of information. He analyzes in detail some typical experiments designed to supply information of a certain kind. He shows that the increase ΔS in the total entropy of the physical system to be investigated together with

---

[3] L. Szilard, "Über die Entropieverminderung in einem thermodynamischen System bei Eingriffen intelligenter Wesen," *Zeitschr. f. Physik* 53 (1929), 840–856.

[4] J. C. Maxwell, *Theory of Heat* (London: Longmans, Green, 1871); p. 328.

[5] L. Brillouin, (1) "Maxwell's demon cannot operate: Information and Entropy I, *J. Applied Physics*," 22 (1951), 334–337. (2) "Physical entropy and information II," *ibid.*, 338–343. (3) "The negentropy principle of information," *ibid.*, 24 (1953), 1152–1163.

the surrounding experimental arrangements can never be less than the increase Δ inf in the amount of information; in other words, the efficiency ε of the experiment, defined as Δ inf/ΔS, is always ≤ 1 (or $\leq k \ln 2$, if Boltzmann's S_B is used and inf is defined by (10-1), compare (10-3)). These and other results of Brillouin's are certainly interesting and clarify the situation with respect to Maxwell's paradox in the direction first suggested by Szilard. However, when Brillouin proceeds to identify negentropy with amount of information, I cannot follow him any longer. He defines entropy by $k \ln P$, where P is the number of "possible structures" or "possible states" or "complexions"; thus he means presumably something like S_B^{II} (6-11) (omitting the additive constant, as is frequently done). At any rate, it seems from his discussions that he implicitly uses what we have called Method II. He does not seem to be aware that the definition of S which he uses (and which he ascribes to Boltzmann and Planck) makes S a logical rather than a physical concept.

Essay II: An Abstract Concept of Entropy and Its use in Inductive Logic

Summary. The aim is to construct an abstract concept of entropy and, with its help, a concept of degree of confirmation, applicable to any system of N elements of any kind which are characterized by quantitative magnitudes. As a preliminary for this aim, the following concepts have been defined for a simple classification system: degree of order o^* and degree of confirmation c^* (§2), degree of disorder d^* and entropy S^* (§3). Then the abstract concept S^{**} for elements with quantitative magnitudes is defined. The definition is given first in a more general form with weights assigned to the elements (§11) and then in a simpler form without weights (§12). On the basis of S^{**}, we define the degree of disorder d^{**}, the degree of order o^{**}, the probability density ϑ, the measure function m^{**}, and finally the degree of confirmation c^{**} (§13). These definitions are such that the relations between these concepts are analogous to the relations between the corresponding concepts for a simple classification (§§2, 3). However, in distinction to the earlier c^*, c^{**} is applicable to our present systems involving quantitative magnitudes. Theorems of inductive logic concerning ϑ and c^{**} are developed in greater detail for a schema with only one magnitude (§§14, 15).

11
The abstract concept of entropy

Summary. We use here the concepts explained in §1. Each element a_i ($i = 1, \ldots, N$) is represented by its phase point b_i in the μ-space. We assign to each phase point b_i an environment e_i such that every point in the μ-space belongs to the environment of the nearest phase point ((11-6), fig. 1). By the use of these environments Boltzmann's cell system becomes unnecessary. Thus the D^{st} and the D^{ind} drop out and we have to deal only with D^{prec}. But our definitions will refer to the precise propositions p^{prec}, i.e. to the systems of values u_{ij}, rather than to the D^{prec}, because not all of the p^{prec} are expressible by D^{prec}. A modified version S'_B of Boltzmann's S_B is defined in terms of the environments (11-9); S'_B is a continuous function of the values u_{ij}. Our abstract concept of entropy S^{**} is defined (11-10) in analogy to Boltzmann's concept. For greater generality, this definition permits the assignment of different weights to the elements. (The second part of this section involving weights may be skipped, because later we shall use chiefly the simple schema without weights dealt with in §12.)

We go back to the concepts explained in §1. They refer to a system of N elements a_i ($i = 1, \ldots, N$), each characterized by the values of n magnitudes ϕ_j ($j = 1, \ldots, n$), with $\phi_j(a_i) = u_{ij}$. The nature of the elements is not specified; they need not be molecules or other physical particles; they may be entities of any kind whatever. Each element a_i is represented by its phase point b_i in the n-dimensional μ-space. R^μ is the total range, i.e., the region of admitted phase points. It has a finite volume V^μ. We make the assumption:

(11-1) No two distinct elements have exactly the same values of all n magnitudes. Hence distinct elements have distinct phase points.

This assumption is certainly fulfilled if the elements are physical bodies or particles at a given time t_1 and the magnitudes include the coordinates of position at t_1 (as in the Boltzmann case).

Boltzmann[1] considers the state of a gas body g at a given time t. g consists of N molecules, each characterized by n magnitudes ϕ_j. This is a special case of the kind explained in §1; but Boltzmann transforms it by the introduction of a cell system into a classification system (as discussed in §§2 and 3). For each magnitude ϕ_j, its interval of admitted values is divided into small intervals of equal length Δ_j. Hereby the μ-space is divided into a system Ω^μ of *cells* of equal volume $v^\mu = \Delta_1 \ldots \Delta_n$. Let K be the number of these cells within the total range R^μ; then:

$$v^\mu = \frac{V^\mu}{K}.$$

These μ-cells Q_j ($j = 1, \ldots, K$) are analogous to the cells Q_j in the classification system (§2).

The introduction of the system of cells is a very ingenious device by which Boltzmann transforms the problem of defining entropy within the framework of the kinetic theory into a problem concerning the simple schema of a K-fold classification. While in the kinetic theory (in its classical form) the possible states constitute an infinite and even non-denumerable set, in the K-schema the number of D^{st} and even that of D^{ind} is finite.

Let f_j be the density in Q_j, i.e., the number of molecules per unit of μ-volume:

$$f_j =_{Df} \frac{N_j}{v^\mu}.$$

Boltzmann defines his entropy concept, which we denote by 'S_B,' for a given D_i^{st} with cell numbers N_j as follows:

(11-2) $$S_B(D_i^{st}) =_{Df} -k \sum_{j=1}^{K} [f_j \ln f_j] v^\mu,$$

where $k = 1.38 \times 10^{-16}$ erg/°C.

We have, as is customary, assumed that the cells Q_j in the μ-space have equal volumes v^μ. However, this assumption is not necessary. We could use cells Q_j with different volumes v_j and replace 'v^μ' in the definition of S_B by 'v_j' and define 'f_j' by 'N_j/v_j.' Suppose that two cells Q'_j and Q''_j with equal densities $f' = f''$ are merged into one new cell Q_j with $v_j = v'_j + v''_j$ (v'_j and v''_j need not be equal) and $N_j = N'_j + N''_j$. Then in Q_j, $f = f' = f''$. The two terms $(f' \ln f') v'_j$ and $(f'' \ln f'') v''_j$ in the $\sum$ for the first system are replaced for the second system by one term $(f \ln f) v_j$, which is equal to the sum of the two terms. Thus $\sum$ and S_B remain unchanged.

The definition of our abstract concept S^{**} will be made analogous to Boltzmann's definition for S_B. It will differ from the latter only in the way of dividing R^μ into parts. Boltzmann chooses an arbitrary number K of parts (cells) of equal volume v^μ; then the

---

[1] L. Boltzmann, *Vorlesungen ueber Gastheorie*, Teil I (Leipzig: J. A. Barth, 1896).

density f_i is N_i/v^μ. We choose instead a fixed equal number of phase points in each part, namely one; that is, we assign to each phase point b_i a part of R^μ containing it, which we call the *environment* e_i of b_i. The volumes v_i of different environments will in general be different. Then the density in e_i could be taken as $1/v_i$ (this will later be modified).

We shall soon give a definition of the environments e_i for a given system. The choice of the particular definition is not important, but it is essential that any system of environments e_i fulfill the following conditions:

(11-3) (a) Every e_i ($i = 1, \ldots, N$) is a subset of R^μ.
(b) For every e_i, its volume $v_i > 0$.
(c) The environments of two distinct phase points do not overlap.
(d) Almost every point of R^μ (i.e., every point with the possible exception of a set of points of measure 0) belongs to one of the N environments; hence $\sum_{i=1}^{N} v_i = V^\mu$.

Let x and x' be two points in the μ-space; let u_j ($j = 1, \ldots, n$) be the coordinates of x and u'_j those of x'. We define the *distance D* in the usual pythagorean form:

(11-4) $$D^2(x, x') =_{Df} \sum_{j=1}^{n} (u_j - u'_j)^2.$$

From (11-1)

(11-5) The distance of the phase points of two distinct elements is > 0.

We now define the environments in terms of distances:

(11-6) The *environment* e_i of the phase point $b_i =_{Df}$ the set of those points X of R^μ for which the distance between X and b_i is smaller than the distance between X and any other of the N phase points.

The *diagram* (fig. 1) represents a two-dimensional μ-space. The rectangular area within the heavy line represents the total range R^μ. It is divided into smaller areas representing the environments; each contains a dot representing one of the N phase points b_i. In

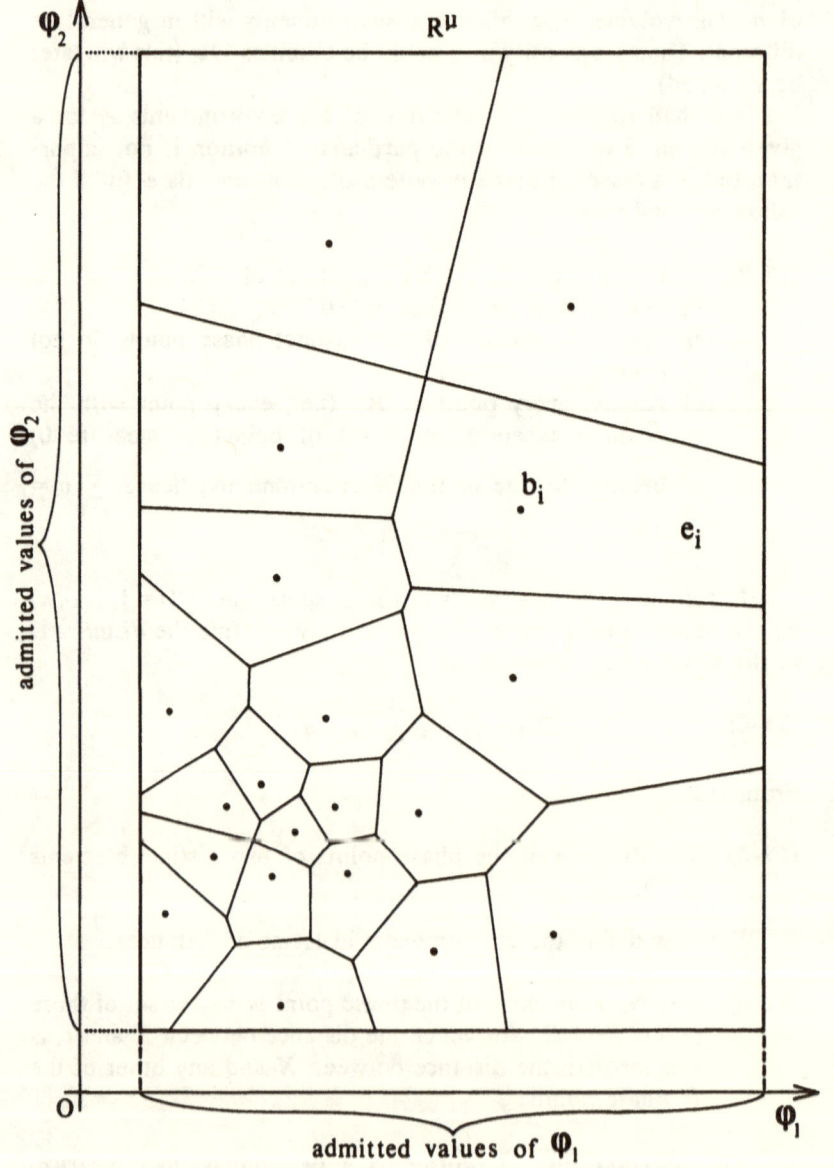

Figure 1. Environments in a 2-dimensional phase space.

accordance with the definition (11-6), in this diagram a segment marking the boundary between the environments e_i of b_i and e'_i of b'_i is part of the straight line which is the perpendicular bisector of the segment $b_i b'_i$. Analogously, in the n-dimensional μ-space, the boundaries between environments are parts of $(n-1)$-dimensional hyperplanes which bisect perpendicularly the segments between two phase points. Consequently, the set of all boundary points (which are the points equidistant from the two nearest phase points) has measure 0; thus the requirement (d) in (11-3) is fulfilled. It is easily seen that the same holds for (a), (b), and (c); (b) follows from (11-5) because the number N of phase points is finite.

In order to make our schema more general, we shall admit the possibility that to each element a_i a positive real number w_i is assigned as its *weight*. For example, the assignment of weight 3 to a_1 and of the weight 5 to a_2 would mean that, in the calculation of densities in the regions of phase space and then of the entropy and of derivative magnitudes, we are to proceed as if there were not one element with the characteristics of a_1 but three, and not one but five with those of a_2; or six like a_1 and ten like a_2, etc. Thus all that matters are the ratios of the weights, not their absolute values. We normalize the weights in such a way that the mean weight is 1; hence:

(11-7) $$\sum_{i=1}^{N} w_i = N.$$

Then we define density thus:

(11-8) $$f_i =_{\text{Df}} w_i / v_i.$$

The sum in the definition of S_B will therefore be replaced by

$$\sum_{i=1}^{N} \left[\frac{w_i}{v_i} \ln \left(\frac{w_i}{v_i} \right) \right] v_i = \sum_i \left[w_i \ln \frac{w_i}{v_i} \right].$$

While Boltzmann's definitions of S_B referred to cell numbers N_j and were applied to D^{st}, our definitions for S^{**} and other concepts will refer only to the environment volumes v_i. Thus we have here no longer to do with D^{st} or D^{ind}, but only with D^{prec}. A D^{prec} is supposed to be a description or statement, formulated in the language, say, of physics, which gives for each element a_i and each function ϕ_j the value $\phi_j(a_i) = u_{ij}$. However, a language system cannot possibly contain expressions for all real numbers of a given interval; therefore it cannot contain D^{prec} for all possible value sets

u_{ij}. Since these value sets are the arguments of our basic concepts, we shall draw the practical consequence from this limitation of all language systems. We shall not refer any longer to D^{prec} but instead to the *precise propositions*, p^{prec}, i.e., the possible value sets u_{ij} themselves. In any given language system, some p^{prec} can be expressed by D^{prec} while all the others are inexpressible. Thus we shall henceforth speak of all p^{prec} for a given system of N elements a_i and n functions ϕ_j without regard to expressibility, just as a theorem of classical mathematics refers to all real numbers without discrimination between those which are expressible in a given language system and those which are not.

For the special case of Boltzmann's theory for a homogeneous gas, we take simply $w_i = 1$. Then we obtain the following definition for an alternative S'_B to Boltzmann's S_B:

(11-9) $$S'_B(p^{\text{prec}}) =_{\text{Df}} k \sum_i \ln v_i.$$

In distinction to S_B, this concept S'_B is not based on an arbitrary cell system and is a continuous function of the u_{ij}.

Since the abstract concept is not restricted to gas molecules but intended to be applicable to arbitrary elements, we may replace in its definition Boltzmann's gas constant k by an arbitrary constant A (>0). For our version S^{**} we choose $A = 1/\ln 2$, as we did for S^* (3-23). One might consider to insert into the definition an additive constant, possibly dependent on N and V^u. We shall, however, not do so, for the following reason. With respect to the definitions to be given in §13, the insertion would result in the appearance of a constant factor in the definitions of o^{**}; but the definition of ϑ would remain unchanged because of the normalization condition (13-13), and hence also the definitions of m^{**} and c^{**}. Therefore we define the *abstract entropy concept* S^{**} as follows:

(11-10) $$S^{**}(p_k^{\text{prec}}) =_{\text{Df}} \sum_{i=1}^{N} \left[w_i \operatorname{Log} \frac{v_i}{w_i} \right]$$

(where 'Log' denotes the logarithm to base 2).

$S^{**}(p_k^{\text{prec}})$ is a continuous function of the N values v_i, and each of these values in turn is a continuous function of the nN values u_{ij}. [The latter would not be the case if a phase point could not only approach another one at any arbitrarily small distance, but could finally coincide with it; this, however, is excluded by our assumption (11-1).]

The entropy $S^{**}(p_k^{\text{prec}})$ may be regarded as the sum of N unequal parts, each attributed to one element. We define the *partial* *entropy of an element* a_i with respect to a given p_k^{prec} as:

(11-11) $$S_{\text{el}}^{**}(a_i, p_k^{\text{prec}}) =_{\text{Df}} w_i \operatorname{Log} \frac{v_i}{w_i}.$$

Then we have:

(11-12) $$S^{**}(p_k^{\text{prec}}) = \sum_i S_{\text{el}}^{**}(a_i, p_k^{\text{prec}}).$$

Let the region R_j be a part of R^μ consisting of N_j environments e_{ji} ($i=1,\ldots,N_j$) with volumes v_{ji} and weights w_{ji}, with respect to a given p_k^{prec}. Then the *partial entropy* of R_j with respect to p_k^{prec} is defined as follows:

(11-13) $$S_{\text{part}}^{**}(R_j, p_k^{\text{prec}}) =_{\text{Df}} \sum_{i=1}^{N_j} \left[w_{ji} \operatorname{Log} \frac{v_{ji}}{w_{ji}} \right].$$

If R^μ consists of K non-overlapping regions R_j ($j=1,\ldots,K$) we have:

(11-14) $$S^{**}(p_k^{\text{prec}}) = \sum_{j=1}^{K} S_{\text{part}}^{**}(R_j, p_k^{\text{prec}}).$$

If R_j is a region as above, its volume is

(11-15) $$V_j = \sum_{i=1}^{N_j} v_{ji},$$

and its weight is

(11-16) $$W_j = \sum_{i=1}^{N_j} w_{ji}.$$

Now suppose that R_j is such that the density f has the same value throughout R_j; in other words, the v_{ji} are proportional to the weights w_{ji}; say for every i from 1 to m_j, $v_{ji} = Cw_{ji}$. Then $V_j = \sum Cw_{ji} = CW_j$. Hence $v_{ji}/w_{ji} = C = V_j/W_j$. Thus with (11-13) and (11-16):

(11-17) $$S_{\text{part}}^{**}(R_j, p_k^{\text{prec}}) = W_j \operatorname{Log} \frac{V_j}{W_j}.$$

We denote the mean environment volume by $\bar{v}$:

(11-18) $$\bar{v} =_{\text{Df}} \frac{V^\mu}{N}.$$

S^{**} has its maximum if the density f_i is the same throughout R^μ. In this case R^μ is like the R_j in (11-17), with $V_j = V^\mu$ and

$W_j = N$ (11-6). Hence:

(11-19) $$S^{**}_{\max} = N \operatorname{Log} \frac{V^\mu}{N} = N \operatorname{Log} \bar{v}.$$

Suppose that with respect to a given p_k^{prec}, R^μ can be divided into K regions R_j ($j = 1, \ldots, K$) with volumes V_j and weights W_j such that within each of these regions the density f is the same for all environments. Then with (11-14) and (11-17):

(11-20) $$S^{**}(p_k^{\text{prec}}) = \sum_{j=1}^{K} \left[W_j \operatorname{Log} \frac{V_j}{W_j} \right].$$

12
A Simpler Schema Without Weights

Summary. The schema is simplified by abandoning the weights. Then S^{**} is simply the sum of the logarithms of the volumes v_i of the environments e_i (12-2)(a). We compare Boltzmann's S_B, which neglects differences of density within the cells, with our version S'_B, which reflects such differences. It is shown that, if the density is constant within each cell, both functions have the same value.

The assignment of weights to the elements seems desirable only for special purposes. In general, it seems sufficient to use a simpler schema, dropping the weights. This schema may be regarded as a special case of the former one, with all $w_i = 1$. Thus from (11-7):

(12-1) $$f_i = 1/v_i.$$

The definition (4-10) of *the abstract entropy concept* S^{**} becomes now:

(12-2) (a) $$S^{**}(p^{\text{prec}}) =_{\text{Df}} \sum_{i=1}^{N} \text{Log } v_i.$$

(b) $$= \text{Log} \prod_{i=1}^{N} v_i.$$

In the same way we obtain the following definitions from (11-11), (11-13), etc.: The partial entropy of an element:

(12-3) $$S^{**}_{\text{el}}(a_i, p^{\text{prec}}) =_{\text{Df}} \text{Log } v_i.$$

The partial entropy of a region R_j consisting of N_j environments e_{ji} with volumes v_{ji}:

(12-4) $$S^{**}_{\text{part}}(R_j, p_k^{\text{prec}}) =_{\text{Df}} \sum_{i=1}^{N_j} \text{Log } v_{ji}.$$

The theorems (11-12) and (11-14) remain valid, of course.

The case of a region R_j with constant density is simpler here than previously. Here R_j consists of N_j environments of equal volume v_j, and hence has volume $V_j = N_j v_j$. The earlier W_j (11-16) is here N_j. Thus the partial entropy of R_j is now (from (11-17)):

(12-5) $$S^{**}_{\text{part}}(R_j, p_k^{\text{prec}}) = N_j \text{ Log } v_j.$$

(This also follows directly from (12-4).)

Let R^μ consist of K regions R_j ($j = 1, \ldots, K$) such that in each region R_j all N_j environments have the same volume $v_j = V_j/N_j$. Then from (12-5) (in analogy to (11-20)):

(12-6) (a) $\quad S^{**}(p_k^{\text{prec}}) = \sum_{j=1}^{K} \left[N_j \operatorname{Log} \dfrac{V_j}{N_j} \right],$

(b) $\quad\quad\quad\quad = \sum_{j=1}^{K} [N_j \operatorname{Log} v_j].$

In the special case that all $V_j = V^\mu/K$, we have:

(12-7) $\quad\quad S^{**}(p_k^{\text{prec}}) = \sum_{j=1}^{K} \left[N_j \operatorname{Log} \dfrac{V^\mu}{N_j K} \right],$

$\quad\quad\quad\quad = -\sum_j [N_j \operatorname{Log} N_j] + N \operatorname{Log} \dfrac{V^\mu}{K}.$

Analogously, for our version S'_B (11-9) of Boltzmann's concept:

(12-8) $\quad\quad S'_B(p^{\text{prec}}) = -k \left\{ \sum_j [N_j \ln N_j] - N \ln \dfrac{V^\mu}{K} \right\}.$

Boltzmann's cells are regions with equal volume $v^\mu = V^\mu/K$. Thus, comparing (12-8) with (11-2), we see that if the phase points in each cell are uniformly distributed, i.e., have equal environments, then S'_B and S_B (the latter taken for the D^μ corresponding to the given p^{prec}) are exactly equal. If the cell numbers N_j remain the same but the phase points in at least one of the cells are unevenly distributed, then S'_B reflects this fact by having a somewhat smaller value than in the former case. On the other hand S_B remains the same, because it depends merely upon the cell numbers and disregards the distributions within the cells. Thus S'_B reflects more faithfully local changes in the physical state.

S^{**} has its *maximum* if all environments have the same volume $\bar{v} = V^\mu/N$. Hence with (12-2)(a), in agreement with (11-19):

(12-9) $\quad\quad\quad\quad S^{**}_{\max} = N \operatorname{Log} \bar{v}.$

The problem of the *minimum* of S^{**} is more complicated. We saw earlier that z and therefore S^* and S_B have their minimum values if all elements belong to the same cell. With respect to a p^{prec}, there are no cells. But it is easily seen that here S^{**} is smaller the closer the phase points are crowded together. Let us assume that all phase points are compressed into a dense cloud occupying only a very small part of R^μ. Then the environments of the phase points in the interior part R_1 of the cloud, which constitute a great majority, say N_1, have very small volumes v_i. We assume that these volumes are equal, say $= v_1$. Outside of R_1, in the remaining region R_2 with volume $V_2 = V^\mu - V_1$, are only the phase points of the external fringe of the cloud. We assume that their number N_2 is only a very small part of the total; hence $r_2 = N_2/N$ is a very small fraction. Because of their relatively small number it does not matter much for the total S^* whether their v_i-values are equal or not. Therefore we may, for an approximate result, take them as being equal, say $= v_2$. Then $V_2 = N_2 v_2$.

According to (12-5), the partial S^{**} for R_1 is $N_1 \text{Log } v_1 = N(1 - r_2) \text{Log } v_1$. That for R_2 is $N_2 \text{Log } v_2 = N r_2 \text{Log}(V_2/Nr_2) \cong N r_2 \text{Log}(V^\mu/Nr_2)$, because $V_2 \cong V^\mu$. Hence for the total S^{**}:

(12-10) (a) $\quad S^{**} \cong N \left\{ \text{Log } v_1 + r_2 \text{Log} \frac{V^\mu}{Nv_1} + r_2 \text{Log} \frac{1}{r_2} \right\}$,

(b) $\quad \cong N \text{Log } v_1$.

The cruder approximation (b) is obtained by dropping the terms with the factor r_2.

Thus S^{**} is the smaller, the smaller v_1. If the cloud of phase points is further compressed into half its previous volume, then S^{**}, according to (12-10)(b), decreases by N. Now we must distinguish two cases.

1. According to our assumptions, every $v_i > 0$ (11-3)(b). First we consider the case that for given N, n, and V^μ there is no positive lower bound for v_1 (although, of course, in any given p^{prec} there is a positive minimum v_i). Then there is no positive lower bound for S^{**}.

2. Suppose the general schema is such that there is a minimum admissible distance between two phase points and hence a minimum possible v_i, say v_{min}, in other words a minimum cloud volume Nv_{min}. Then there is a minimum for S^{**}; with (12-10)(b):

(12-11) $\quad\quad\quad\quad S^{**}_{min} \cong N \text{Log } v_{min}$.

[We considered above a system, say p_1^{prec}, in which all phase points are concentrated in one cloud. Let us now consider systems p_k^{prec} ($k = 1, 2, \ldots$) with a small number k of separate clouds of equal volume, all with the same v_1 as before. We shall find that $S^{**}(p_k^{prec})$ slightly increases with k, and therefore that among these systems (with given N, n, V^μ, and v_1) p_1^{prec} has the smallest S^{**}. For the sake of simplicity, let us assume that each of the k clouds has the shape of an n-dimensional hypercube and that the phase points are arranged in each cloud in an n-dimensional cubic lattice with distance D. Hence $v_1 = D^n$. Let the number of phase points along each edge of a hypercube be m. (We assume that N/k is sufficiently large so that the difference between it and the nearest nth power of an integer, viz. m^n, may be neglected; and that m is considerably larger than $2n$.) Then each cloud contains m^n phase points. Hence $N = km^n$ and $m = \sqrt[n]{\frac{N}{k}}$. The number of interior phase points in each cloud is $(m-2)^n = m^n \left(1 - \frac{2}{m}\right)^n \cong m^n \left[1 - \frac{2n}{m}\right]$, where $\frac{2n}{m}$ is a small fraction. r_1 is the ratio of interior phase points to all phase points, which is equal to this ratio in each cloud; hence $r_1 \cong 1 - \frac{2n}{m}$. Then $r_2 = 1 - r_1 \cong \frac{2n}{m} \cong \frac{2n\sqrt[n]{k}}{\sqrt[n]{N}}$. Thus r_2 increases slowly with k. Suppose that N, n, V^μ, and v_1 are given. We see from (12-10)(b) that S^{**} is in the first approximation independent of r_2 and hence of k; in other words, dividing the cloud into k separate parts does not make much difference for the value of S^{**}. (12-10)(a) shows that S^{**} increases with r_2 (since $r_2 \text{Log} \frac{1}{r_2}$ increases with r_2 for $r_2 < e^{-1} \approx 0.368$) and hence with k. Thus S^{**} increases slightly if the cloud is divided into separate parts.]

13
Degree of Confirmation

Summary. We defined earlier (§2 and §3) for a classification schema, first the degree of order o^*, then the degree of disorder $d^* = 1/o^*$, and finally the entropy $S^{**} = \text{Log } d^*$ (+ const.). Now, for the quantitative schema, we proceed analogously in the inverse direction. We have defined S^{**}; we now define d^{**} such that $\text{Log } d^{**} = S^{**}$, and $o^{**} = 1/d^{**}$. For the schema without weights (§12), we have simply $o^{**} = \prod_i (1/v_i)$ (13-9). In order to obtain a concept of degree of confirmation c^{**} for quantitative systems analogous to the earlier c^*, we define the probability density ϑ as proportional to o^{**}, then the measure function m^{**} for a proposition p as the integral of ϑ over the range of p in the γ-space, and finally, in the usual way, $c^{**}(h, e)$ as $m^{**}(e \cdot h)/m^{**}(e)$.

Earlier (§3), in the case of a simple classification system, we defined the entropy S^* on the basis of the degree of disorder d^*. Now we have defined the entropy S^{**} for a system involving quantitative magnitudes, without making use of any concept of degree of disorder. However, we can now find a concept d^{**}, the degree of disorder for a quantitative system, by requiring that the relation between S^{**} and d^{**} be analogous to that between S^* and d^*. On the basis of d^{**}, we define the degree of order as its reciprocal and then the degree of confirmation in analogy to the earlier procedure.

S^* was defined in such a way that it was equal to $\text{Log } d^*$, aside from an additive constant dependent upon N and K (see (3-27)). In the case of S^{**}, we might analogously add a constant dependent on N and n. However, the value of this constant is inessential, since it would not influence the value of the degree of confirmation (see (13-17) below). Therefore we shall omit the constant. Thus we wish d^{**} to be such that

$$\text{Log } d^{**}(p_k^{\text{prec}}) = S^{**}(p_k^{\text{prec}}),$$

$$= \sum_{i=1}^{N} \left[w_i \text{ Log } \frac{v_i}{w_i} \right] \quad (11\text{-}10)$$

$$= \text{Log } \prod_i \left(\frac{v_i}{w_i} \right)^{w_i}.$$

Therefore we define the *degree of disorder*:

(13-1) $$d^{**}(p_k^{\text{prec}}) =_{\text{Df}} \prod_{i=1}^{N} \left(\frac{v_i}{w_i} \right)^{w_i}.$$

d^{**} has, like S^{**}, its maximum if the density is the same throughout R^u. Therefore, with (11-19):

(13-2) $$d^{**}_{\max} = \bar{v}^N, \quad \text{where} \quad \bar{v} = V^u/N.$$

For the schema without weights (i.e., $w_i = 1$, §12):

(13-3) $$d^{**}(p_k^{\text{prec}}) =_{\text{Df}} \prod_i v_i.$$

If r^u consists of K regions $R_j (j = 1, \ldots, K)$ such that in R_j all N_j environments have the same volume v_j, we have:

(13-4) $$d^{**}(p_k^{\text{prec}}) = \prod_{j=1}^{K} v_j^{N_j}.$$

If all phase points are concentrated in a cloud of small volume V_c with equal density, then approximately (from (12-10)(b)):

(13-5) $$d^{**} \cong v_1^N, \quad \text{where} \quad v_1 = \frac{V_c}{N}.$$

If the schema is such that there is a minimum $v_{\min}$ for the possible environment volumes v_i, then according to (13-5):

(13-6) $$d^{**}_{\min} \cong v_{\min}^N.$$

If there is no positive lower bound for the possible v_i, then d^{**} has no minimum, and its greatest lower bound is 0.

Originally we defined disorder as the reciprocal of order (3-1). Thus now we take o^{**} as the reciprocal of d^{**}:

(13-7) $$o^{**}(p_k^{\text{prec}}) =_{\text{Df}} \frac{1}{d^{**}(p^{\text{prec}})}.$$

Hence we have for a system with weights:

(13-8) $$o^{**}(p_k^{\text{prec}}) = \prod_{i=1}^{N} \left(\frac{w_i}{v_i}\right)^{w_i},$$

and for a system without weights:

(13-9) $$o^{**}(p_k^{\text{prec}}) = \prod_{i=1}^{N} \frac{1}{v_i}.$$

From (13-2):

(13-10) $\quad o^{**}_{\min} = \left(\dfrac{1}{\bar{v}}\right)^N,\quad$ where $\bar{v} = V^\mu/N$.

If there is a minimum $v_{\min}$ of the possible v_i-values, then

(13-11) $\quad o^{**}_{\max} = \left(\dfrac{1}{v_{\min}}\right)^N.$

Otherwise there is no maximum of o^{**}. If the volume of concentration V_c is compressed to $1/m$ of its previous value, o^{**} is multiplied by approximately m^N (from (13-5)).

Now we come to the problem of defining a concept of degree of confirmation c^{**} for our quantitative systems. c^{**} will be based in the customary way on a measure function m^{**} which represents the initial degree of confirmation. For classification systems (§2) we defined m^* as proportional to the degree of order o^*. For the quantitative systems, we have defined a degree of order o^{**}, and therefore we shall proceed here in a similar way. However, in the present case the situation is somewhat more complicated. The number of possible D^{ind} in a classification schema with given N and K was finite; therefore we could simply ascribe values of m^* to the D^{ind} in such a way that the sum of all these values was 1. This is not possible for the p^{prec} in a quantitative schema, because they form a continuum. Therefore we must ascribe to them values of an m-density function ϑ such that the integral of ϑ over the whole continuum is 1. We shall take ϑ to be proportional to o^{**}.

Previously we represented each of the N elements a_i, characterized by the n values $u_{i1}, \ldots, u_{in}$, by a phase point in the n-dimensional μ-space (molecule-space). Following Gibbs, we introduce now a second phase-space, the so-called γ-*space* (gas-space). In this Nn-dimensional space the whole system of N elements, characterized by the Nn values $u_{11}, \ldots, u_{1n}, u_{21}, \ldots, u_{2n}, \ldots, u_{N1}, \ldots, u_{Nn}$, in other words, the p^{prec}, is represented by one point. We shall use 'U' as a variable for an ordered set of Nn values $u_{11}, \ldots, u_{Nn}$ as coordinates and hence for a point in the γ-space. The total range R^μ in the μ-space determines the total range R^γ in the γ-space. Let V^γ be the (Nn-dimensional) volume of R^γ; then $V^\gamma = (V^\mu)^N$.

The values of the function $o^{**}(p^{\text{prec}})$ will also be assigned to the phase points U representing the p^{prec}. Thus we shall have a function $o^{**}(U)$ in the γ-space. The density function δ to be defined may likewise be regarded as a function $\delta(U)$ in the γ-space.

Now we define δ as proportional to o^{**}:

(13-12) (a) For a point U in R^γ, $\quad \delta(U) =_{Df} Co^{**}(U)$.

(b) For a point U outside of R^γ, $\quad \delta(U) =_{Df} 0$.

The proportionality factor C, possibly dependent upon N, n, and V^μ, but not on U, is uniquely determined by the normalization requirement previously mentioned:

$$\text{(13-13)} \qquad \int_{R^\gamma} \delta(U) \, dU = 1,$$

where $dU = du_{11} \ldots du_{Nn}$ is a volume differential in the γ-space, and the integral runs over R^γ (or over the whole γ-space; this makes no difference because of (13-12)(b)). With (13-12a):

$$\text{(13-14)} \qquad C \int_{R^\gamma} o^{**}(U) \, dU = 1,$$

hence:

$$\text{(13-15)} \qquad C = \frac{1}{\int_{R^\gamma} o^{**}(U) \, dU}.$$

From (13-12)(a):

(13-16) For any U in R^γ, $\delta(U) =_{Df} \dfrac{o^{**}(U)}{\int_{R^\gamma} o^{**}(U) \, dU}$.

We shall now prove two results (13-17) and (13-18) concerning the *invariance of* δ under certain conditions. The results show likewise the invariance of m^{**} and c^{**}, because these functions will be defined on the basis of δ. The results hold both for the schema with weights and for that without weights.

(13-17) If $S^{**\prime} = S^{**} + B$, where the additive constant B depends at most on N, n, and V^μ, and if $d^{**\prime}$, $o^{**\prime}$, and δ' are defined on $S^{**\prime}$ as d^{**}, o^{**}, and δ were on S^{**}, then δ' and δ coincide.

Proof. Log $d^{**\prime} = S^{**\prime} = S^{**} + B$. Hence $d^{**\prime} = 2^{S^{**}+B} = 2^B d^{**}$. Hence $o^{**\prime} = o^{**}/2^B$. The factor $1/2^B$ cancels out in (13-16), thus δ remains unchanged.

(13-18) δ is invariant with respect to any linear transformation of any of the magnitudes ϕ_j.

Proof. Consider, as an example, ϕ_1. Let $\phi'_1(a_i) =_{\text{Df}} A_1\phi_1(a_i) + A_0$. This means a change in the scale of ϕ_1 with the new unit being $1/A_1$ times the original unit and the zero point shifted by the amount A_0. The difference in ϕ_1 for any two phase points of elements in the μ-space is hereby multiplied by A_1. Therefore v_i is replaced by $v'_i = A_1 v_i$. [In the earlier diagram (fig. 1, in §11), the change may be represented either by shifting the zero point of ϕ_1 by A_0 to the left and taking a new unit $1/A_1$ times the original unit, or by leaving the scale on the ϕ_1-axis intact but shifting the whole diagram to the right and extending it A_1 times in the ϕ_1-direction.] Thus in (11-10) $w_i \text{Log} \frac{v_i}{w_i}$ is replaced by $w_i \text{Log} \frac{A_1 v_i}{w_i} = w_i \text{Log} \frac{v_i}{w_i} + w_i \text{Log} A_1$. Therefore S^{**} is increased by $\sum (w_i \text{Log} A_1) = N \text{Log} A_1$ (from (11-6)). The same result holds for the schema without weights. Hence the assertion with (13-17).

It is important that the invariance (13-18) holds for any one of the magnitudes ϕ_j separately. Thus δ is independent of the more or less arbitrary relations which may hold between the units chosen for different magnitudes. δ is still affected by a change in the scale form of a magnitude ϕ_j, i.e., by a nonlinear transformation. This seems inevitable.

The definition (13-16) for δ can, if desired, be applied to the general schema with weights by using for o^{**} the definition (13-8). We shall, however, *develop our inductive method only for the simple schema without weights*, using (13-9).

The environment volumes $v_1, \ldots, v_N$ in the μ-space depend upon the set of values $U = \{u_{11}, \ldots, u_{Nn}\}$ and may therefore be regarded as functions of $U: v_1(U), \ldots, v_N(U)$. We introduce for abbreviation the function sign $\prod$:

(13-19) $$\prod(U) =_{\text{Df}} \prod_{i=1}^{N} \frac{1}{v_i(U)}.$$

For any subset α of the γ-space, we put

(13-20) $$I(\alpha) =_{\text{Df}} \int_\alpha \prod(U) \, dU, \quad = \int_\alpha \prod_{i=1}^{N} \frac{1}{v_i(U)} \, dU.$$

From (13-16) and (13-9):

(13-21) For any U in R^γ, $\delta(U) = \dfrac{\prod(U)}{I(R)}.$

Let p be any proposition in the given schema, i.e., concerning the n elements and the n magnitudes ϕ_j. By the *range of* p we understood the set of those p^{prec} in which p holds, or the set R_p of the corresponding phase points in the γ-space. [For the reasons given in §11, we refer here to propositions and not to sentences, as in (Prob.).]

Then we define:

(13-22) $$m^{**}(p) =_{\text{Df}} \int_{R_p} \delta(U)\, dU.$$

Hence

(13-23) $$m^{**}(p) = \frac{I(R_p)}{I(R^\delta)}.$$

We define c^* in the customary way (see (2-9)):

(13-24) $$c^{**}(h, e) =_{\text{Df}} \frac{m^{**}(e \cdot h)}{m^{**}(e)}$$

Hence

(13-25) $$c^{**}(h, e) = \frac{I(R_e \cdot h)}{I(R_e)}.$$

Suppose that the evidence e is such that for one (or several) of the magnitudes u_{ij} only a finite number of values are compatible with e. Then $I(R_e) = 0$ and, for any h, $I(R_e \cdot h) = 0$. Thus (13-25) would yield 0/0; this means that the given definitions are not applicable in this case. The following procedure leads still to a definite c^{**}-value in many cases of this kind. Let $e_{I(\alpha)}$, where α is a subset of R_e, be formed by modifying (13-20) as follows: in the multiple integral, the integral for each magnitude u_{ij} which is confined in e to a finite number of values is replaced by a sum running through these values, and the corresponding differential in dU is dropped; if only one value of a magnitude is compatible with e, this value is substituted in $\Pi(U)$ and no sum is applied. Then the following definitions are used; they are modifications of (13-21) and (13-25), respectively:

(13-26) For any U in R_e, ${}^e\delta(U) =_{\text{Df}} \dfrac{\Pi(U)}{{}^eI(R_e)}.$

(13-27) $$c^{**}(h, e) =_{\text{Df}} \frac{{}^eI(R_e \cdot h)}{{}^eI(R_e)}.$$

This procedure will be applied in the next section.

14
Application to a schema with one magnitude

Summary. The concepts defined in the preceding section are now applied to the following case. The N elements are characterized by the values of only one magnitude ϕ_1. The evidence e specifies the values $c_1, \ldots, c_{N-1}$ of ϕ_1 for $a_1, \ldots, a_{N-1}$, respectively. The value u for a_N is unknown. Theorems about the following values are stated: $o^{**} = \prod_i (1/v_i)$, now taken as a function $\prod(u)$, and a modified form $\prod'(u)$; the probability density $\delta(u)$ and a modified form $'\delta(u)$; c^{**}, with respect to the given evidence, for various hypotheses concerning u, among them the hypothesis that u lies within the interval $R_k = (c_k, c_{k+1})$.

We shall now apply the concept of degree of confirmation c^{**} defined in the preceding section to a schema with $n = 1$, i.e., with only one magnitude ϕ_1. Let the interval of admitted values of ϕ_1 be the open interval (A, B).

Throughout our further discussion (§§14, 15), we presuppose a fixed evidence e which specifies fixed values of ϕ_1 for all elements except the last one, a_N:

(14-1) $\phi_1(a_1) = c_1; \phi_1(a_2) = c_2; \ldots; \phi_1(a_{N-1}) = c_{N-1}$.

The ϕ_1-values for distinct elements are distinct from one another (11-1) and from A and B. But we assume that the difference between two ϕ_1-values, or between a ϕ_1-value and A or B may be arbitrarily small. We assume further that the values $c_1, \ldots, c_{N-1}$ are in ascending order:

(14-2) $A < c_1 < c_2 \ldots c_i < c_{i+1} \ldots c_{N-2} < c_{N-1} < B$.

Thus the only value left undetermined in e is $\phi_1(a_N)$. We shall use for this value the variable u, which is restricted as follows:

(14-3) (a) $A < u < B$.
       (b) $u \neq c_1, \ldots, c_{N-1}$.

On the basis of the given e, U is the value system $\{c_1, \ldots, c_{N-1}, u\}$, where only the last value can vary. Therefore, as an argument expression for a function, we shall often simply write 'u' instead of '$c_1, \ldots, c_{N-1}, u$' or 'U' e.g. '$v_i(u)$,' '$\prod(u)$,' '$\delta(u)$,' etc. Thus (6-19) with (6-9) now becomes:

(14-4) $$o^{**}(u) = \Pi(u) = \prod_{i=1}^{N} \frac{1}{v_i(u)}.$$

The μ-space here is one-dimensional and the γ-space N-dimensional. However, although R^γ is an N-dimensional region in the γ-space, R_e is only a one-dimensional subset of R^γ. The first $N-1$ coordinates in R_e are fixed as $c_1, \ldots, c_{N-1}$, and R_e is simply the segment (A, B) of the Nth coordinate. The N-dimensional volume of R_e is 0, hence $I(R_e) = 0$. Therefore, to avoid the result 0/0, we must apply here the procedure explained at the end of the preceding section. We form $'I(\alpha)$ by dropping in (13-20) the first $N-1$ integrals and differentials, leaving only those with u; no sums are needed here, since for each a_i ($i = 1$ to $N-1$) one value of ϕ_1 is fixed in e. Thus we have:

(14-5) For any subset α of R_e,

$$'I(\alpha) =_{Df} \int_{u \text{ in } \alpha} \Pi(u)\, du$$
$$= \int \left(\prod_{i=1}^{N} \frac{1}{v_i(u)} \right) du$$

Then (13-26) and (13-27) can be applied. To the values $c_1, \ldots, c_{N-1}$ we add two fictitious ones, for simplifying formulas: c_0 for the mirror image of c_1 with respect to A, and c_N for the mirror image of c_{N-1} with respect to B (see the diagram; note that the coordinate of a_N is not c_N, but rather u):

(14-6) (a) $c_0 =_{Df} 2A - c_1$.
(b) $c_N =_{Df} 2B - c_{N-1}$.

The *diagram* (fig. 2) shows the one-dimensional μ-space. The total range R^μ is the interval (A, B), represented by a heavy line. We introduce a notation '$R..$' for some open subinterval and '$D..$' for

	c_0	A	c_1	c_2	...	c_k	c_{k+1}	...	c_{N-2}	c_{N-1}	B		c_N
Intervals:		R_0 (R_A)	R_1			R_k			R_{N-2}	(R_B)		R_{N-1}	
Lengths:		D_0 (D_A)	D_1			D_k			D_{N-2}	(D_B)		D_{N-1}	

Figure 2. Fixed points and intervals given by e.

their lengths:

(14-7) (a) For $i=0,\ldots,N-1$, $R_i =_{Df} (c_i, c_{i+1})$.
 (b) $R_A =_{Df} (A, c_1)$.
 (c) $R_B =_{Df} (c_{N-1}, B)$.

(14-8) (a) For $i=0,\ldots,N-1$, $D_i =_{Df} c_{i+1} - c_i$.
 (b) $D_A =_{Df} c_1 - A = \frac{1}{2} D_0$.
 (c) $D_B =_{Df} B - c_{N-1} = \frac{1}{2} D_{N-1}$.

We further introduce "$^e v_i$" ($i=1,\ldots,N-1$), where 'e' refers to the given evidence, as auxiliary terms for our calculations. $^e v_i$ is, so to speak, the volume of the fictitious environment which the phase point a_i would have on the basis of the evidence e alone, i.e., if the elements $a_1,\ldots,a_{N-1}$ as described in e were the only elements. In this fictitious case, according to (11-5), the environment corresponding to a_i would be the interval $\left(\frac{c_{i-1}+c_i}{2}, \frac{c_i+c_{i+1}}{2}\right)$. (Because of (14-6), this holds also for $i=1$ and $i=N-1$.) Therefore we define:

(14-9) For $i=1,\ldots,N-1$, $^e v_i =_{Df} \frac{1}{2}(c_{i+1}-c_{i-1}) = \frac{1}{2}(D_{i-1}+D_i)$.

In terms of these fictitious volumes we define:

(14-10) $$\Pi_e =_{Df} \prod_{i=1}^{N-1} \frac{1}{^e v_i} = \frac{2^{N-1}}{\prod_{i=1}^{N-1} (D_{i-1}+D_i)}.$$

Now we shall study the various possibilities for $\phi_1(a_N) = u$. First we consider the case that u lies in a given interval R_k, i.e., $c_k < u < c_{k+1}$ ($k=1,\ldots,N-2$). In this case, for every i from 1 to $N-1$, except for $i=k$ and $i=k+1$, $v_i(u) = {^e v_i}$. But instead of the two fictitious volumes $^e v_k$ and $^e v_{k+1}$, we have here three actual ones, viz. $v_k(u) = \frac{1}{2}(u - c_{k-1})$, $v_N(u) = \frac{1}{2}(c_{k+1}-c_k) = \frac{1}{2}D_k$, and $v_{k+1}(u) = \frac{1}{2}(c_{k+2}-u)$; see the diagram (fig. 3).

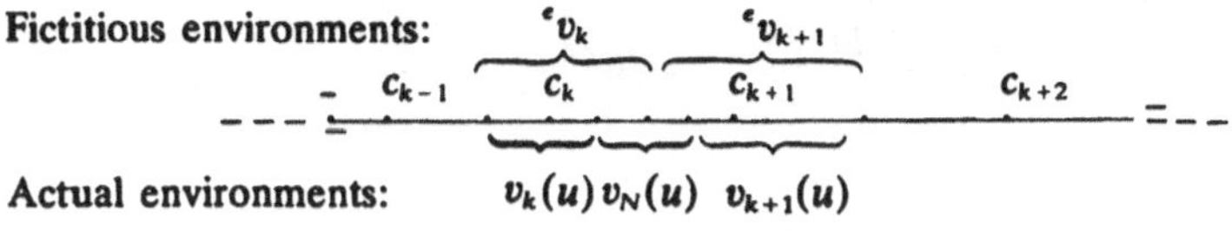

Fictitious environments: $^e v_k$ $^e v_{k+1}$

c_{k-1} c_k c_{k+1} c_{k+2}

Actual environments: $v_k(u)$ $v_N(u)$ $v_{k+1}(u)$

Figure 3. Fictitious and actual environments.

Thus $\Pi(u)$ can now be obtained as a modification of Π_e (14-10):

(14-11) For any u in R_k ($k=1,\ldots,N-2$),

$$\Pi(u) = \Pi_e \cdot \frac{{}^e v_k \cdot {}^e v_{k+1}}{v_k(u) \cdot v_N(u) \cdot v_{k+1}(u)}$$

$$= \Pi_e \cdot \frac{2(c_{k+1} - c_{k-1})(c_{k+2} - c_k)}{(u - c_{k-1})(c_{k+1} - c_k)(c_{k+2} - u)}$$

$$= 2\Pi_e \cdot \frac{(D_{k-1} + D_k)(D_k + D_{k+1})}{(u - c_{k-1}) D_k (c_{k+2} - u)}.$$

Since $\Pi(u)$ and the various values of ${}^{\bullet}I(\alpha)$ contain the factor $2\Pi_e$, it is convenient to put:

(14-12) $$\Pi'(u) =_{\text{Df}} \frac{\Pi(u)}{2\Pi_e},$$

(14-13) $${}^{\bullet}I'(\alpha) =_{\text{Df}} \frac{{}^{\bullet}I(\alpha)}{2\Pi_e}.$$

We shall find that ${}^{\bullet}I'(R_k)$ depends only upon the quotients of the lengths of contiguous intervals, not upon these lengths themselves. Therefore it is convenient to have a notation for these quotients:

(14-14) (a) For $i = 0, \ldots, N-2$, $\quad q_i^+ =_{\text{Df}} \dfrac{D_{i+1}}{D_i}$;

(b) For $i = 1, \ldots, N-1$, $\quad q_i^- =_{\text{Df}} \dfrac{D_{i-1}}{D_i}$;

(c) $q_A^+ =_{\text{Df}} \dfrac{D_1}{D_A} = 2q_0^+$.

(d) $q_B^- =_{\text{Df}} \dfrac{D_{N-2}}{D_B} = 2q_{N-1}^-$.

The following results hold for any R_k ($k=1,\ldots,N-2$). From (14-11)

(14-15) (a) For u in R_k, $\Pi'(u)$

$$= \frac{(D_{k-1} + D_k)(D_k + D_{k+1})}{D_k} \cdot \frac{1}{(u - c_{k-1})(c_{k+2} - u)},$$

(b) $\quad = D_k (1 + q_k^-)(1 + q_k^+) \cdot \dfrac{1}{(u - c_{k-1})(c_{k+2} - u)}$.

From (14-5):

(14-16) For any interval (u', u'') within R_k,

$${}^e I'((u', u'')) = D_k(1+q_k^-)(1+q_k^+)\int_{u'}^{u''} \frac{du}{(u-c_{k-1})(c_{k+2}-u)}.$$

Now we shall use the following indefinite integral:[1]

(14-17) If $W = b^2 - ac > 0$, then

$$\int \frac{dx}{ax^2+2bx+c} = \frac{1}{2\sqrt{W}} \ln\left[C\frac{ax+b-\sqrt{W}}{ax+b+\sqrt{W}}\right].$$

The integral in (14-16) is

$$\int_{u'}^{u''} \frac{du}{-u^2+(c_{k-1}+c_{k+2})u-c_{k-1}c_{k+2}}.$$

Hence $W = \frac{1}{4}(c_{k+2}-c_{k-1})^2 = \frac{1}{4}(D_{k-1}+D_k+D_{k+1})^2 > 0$. Therefore, with (14-17), the integral is

$$\frac{1}{D_{k-1}+D_k+D_{k+1}} \ln\left[\frac{(u''-c_{k-1})(c_{k+1}-u')}{(c_{k+2}-u'')(u'-c_{k-1})}\right].$$

Hence:

(14-18) $\quad {}^e I'((u',u'')) = \dfrac{(1+q_k^-)(1+q_k^+)}{(1+q_k^-+q_k^+)} \ln\left[\dfrac{(u''-c_{k-1})(c_{k+1}-u')}{(c_{k+2}-u'')(u'-c_{k-1})}\right].$

For R_k itself, with $u' = c_k$ and $u'' = c_{k+1}$, the argument of ln in (14-18) becomes

$$\frac{(D_{k-1}+D_k)(D_k+D_{k+1})}{D_{k-1}D_{k+1}};$$

hence:

(14-19) $\quad {}^e I'(R_k) = \dfrac{(1+q_k^-)(1+q_k^+)}{(1+q_k^-+q_k^+)} \ln\left[\left(1+\dfrac{1}{q_k^-}\right)\left(1+\dfrac{1}{q_k^+}\right)\right].$

The results just stated hold for any one of the interior subintervals R_k ($k = 1, \ldots, N-2$). Now we study the two *marginal intervals*. First we consider the case that u lies within R_A, i.e., $A < u < c_1$. Here we have to replace in Π_e the fictitious volume ${}^e v_1 = \frac{1}{2}(D_0+D_1)$

---

[1] W. Gröbner and N. Hofreiter, *Integraltafeln*, (Wien and Innsbruck: Springer-Verlag, 1949), 1:1(7b).

(14-9) by the two actual volumes $v_N(u) = \frac{1}{2}(u+c_1) - A = \frac{1}{2}(u-c_0)$ and $v_1(u) = \frac{1}{2}(c_2-u)$. Therefore, in analogy to (14-11):

(14-20) For any u in R_A,

(a) $\Pi(u) = \Pi_e \cdot \dfrac{{}^e v_1}{v_N(u) \cdot v_1(u)}$.

(b) $\Pi'(u) = \dfrac{D_0 + D_1}{(u-c_0)(c_2-u)}$.

With (14-5) and (14-13):

(14-21) For any interval (u', u'') within R_A,

$${}^e\Gamma((u', u'')) = (D_0 + D_1) \int_{u'}^{u''} \frac{du}{(u-c_0)(c_2-u)}.$$

By (14-17), this integral is

$$\frac{1}{c_2 - c_0} \ln\left[\frac{(u''-c_0)(c_2-u')}{(c_2-u'')(u'-c_0)}\right].$$

Hence:

(14-22) $\quad {}^e\Gamma((u', u'')) = \ln\left[\dfrac{(u''-c_0)(c_2-u')}{(c_2-u'')(u'-c_0)}\right]$.

Hence for R_A itself, with $u' = A$, $u'' = c_1$, and $c_0 = 2A - c_1$ (14-6)(a):

(14-23) $\quad {}^e\Gamma(R_A) = \ln\left[\dfrac{(c_1-c_0)(c_2-A)}{(c_2-c_1)(A-c_0)}\right]$,

$= \ln \dfrac{2(D_A + D_1)}{D_1} = \ln\left[2\left(1 + \dfrac{1}{q_A^+}\right)\right]$.

Analogously for the interval R_B:

(14-24) For any u in R_B,

$$\Pi'(u) = \frac{D_{N-2} + D_{N-1}}{(c_N-u)(u-c_{N-2})}.$$

(14-25) For any interval (u', u'') within R_B,

$${}^e\Gamma((u', u'')) = \ln\left[\frac{(c_N-u')(u''-c_{N-2})}{(u'-c_{N-2})(c_N-u'')}\right].$$

(14-26) $\quad {}^e\Gamma(R_B) = \ln \dfrac{2(D_{N-2} + D_B)}{D_{N-2}} = \ln\left[2\left(1 + \dfrac{1}{q_B^-}\right)\right]$.

'I' for R_e, i.e., for the whole interval (A, B), is the sum of its values for the N subintervals:

(14-27) $\quad {}^eI'(R_A) + {}^eI'(R_B) + \sum_{k=1}^{N-2} {}^eI'(R_k),$

$$= \ln\left[2\left(1+\frac{1}{q_A^+}\right)\right] + \ln\left[2\left(1+\frac{1}{q_B^-}\right)\right]$$

$$+ \sum_{k=1}^{N-2}\left[\frac{(1+q_k^-)(1+q_k^+)}{(1+q_k^-+q_k^+)}\ln\left[\left(1+\frac{1}{q_k^-}\right)\left(1+\frac{1}{q_k^+}\right)\right]\right].$$

For any interval α within (A, B), let $[\alpha]$ be the proposition that the coordinate u of a_N belongs to α. From (13-27):

(14-28) For any intervals α and β within (A, B), β being within α,

$$c^{**}([\beta],[\alpha]) = \frac{{}^eI(\beta)}{{}^eI(\alpha)} = \frac{{}^eI'(\beta)}{{}^eI'(\alpha)}.$$

We have determined the values of ${}^eI'$ for (A, B) (14-27), R_k ($k=1,\ldots,N-2$) (7-19), R_A (14-23), R_B (14-26), and arbitrary subintervals of R_k, R_A, or R_B ((14-18), (14-22), (14-25)). Thus $c^{**}([R_k], e)$, and for any interval β within R_k, $c^{**}([\beta], e)$ and $c^{**}([\beta], [R_k])$, etc. can be determined by (14-28).

From (13-26):

(14-29) For any u in R_e,

$$^e\delta(u) = \frac{\Pi'(u)}{{}^eI'(R_e)}.$$

Thus the m^{**}-density ${}^e\delta$ (with respect to e) is proportional to $\Pi'(u)$. We shall now study the shape of the function $\Pi'(u)$ or of a curve representing it; that will give us a picture of the shape of ${}^e\delta$.

$\Pi'(u)$ within R_k is given by (14-15). Put $f(u) =_{\text{Df}} (u - c_{k-1}) \times (c_{k+2} - u)$. f is 0 for $u = c_{k-1}$ and $u = c_{k+2}$. f has its maximum at the midpoint of c_{k-1} and c_{k+2}; $f_{\max} = \frac{1}{4}(c_{k+2} - c_{k-1})^2 = \frac{1}{4}(D_{k-1} + D_k + D_{k+1})^2 = W_k$. f is represented by a parabola with vertical axis (the dotted line in the *diagram* (fig. 4); the maximum point just mentioned is its vertex. $\Pi'(u)$ is proportional to $\dfrac{1}{f(u)}$. The latter function is still determined by c_{k-1} and c_{k+2} alone. It is indicated in the diagram by the solid and dashed line. $\Pi'(u)$ is furthermore influenced by the values c_k and c_{k+1} in two ways. First, $\dfrac{1}{f(u)}$ is multiplied by $D_k(1+q_k^-)(1+q_k^+)$. Since this is a constant factor, the resulting function may still be regarded as represented by the same curve in the diagram (with a different scale). Second, the positions of c_k and c_{k+1} determine the interval $R_k = (c_k, c_{k+1})$ and thereby that segment of the curve which represents $\Pi'(u)$ in R_k. This segment is the solid part of the curve in the diagram. [The remaining dashed parts do *not* represent $\Pi'(u)$ in the two adjacent intervals; for each interval, $\Pi'(u)$ is to be determined by a new construction of the kind described.]

(14-30) If the midpoint $\tfrac{1}{2}(c_{k-1}+c_{k+2})$ belongs to R_k, then at this point

For a curve representing $\Pi'(u)$ in R_A, according to (14-20)(b), a similar construction would be made over the base (c_0, c_2); analogously for R_B (14-24).

Thus the total curve for $\Pi'(u)$ over (A, B) consists of the N segments described for the intervals $R_A, R_1, \ldots, R_{N-2}, R_B$. The question arises whether these segments join together at their ends or whether there could be jumps at the boundary points. We shall see that there are no jumps, in other words, the function $\Pi'(u)$ is continuous in the following sense. Strictly speaking, the coordinate u of a_N cannot coincide with any of the values c_k (14-3)(b), and $\Pi'(u)$ is therefore not defined for these values. However, since $\Pi'(u)$ is defined for all other values within (A, B), we can determine its limits for any value c_k. Then we find the following:

(14-31) The limits of $\Pi'(u)$ for u approaching a given c_k ($k = 1, \ldots, N-1$) from below and from above are both $= \dfrac{D_{k-1}+D_k}{D_{k-1}D_k}$. Henceforth we shall take this value as the value of Π' for c_k. Then Π' is everywhere continuous.

Proof. (1) For $k = 2, \ldots, N-2$. The limit at c_k from above is found from $\Pi'(u)$ in R_k (14-15) by simply taking $u = c_k$. Hence it is $\dfrac{D_{k-1}+D_k}{D_{k-1}D_k}$.

(2) $\Pi'(u)$ in R_{k-1} is, in analogy to (14-15), equal to $\dfrac{(D_{k-2}+D_{k-1})(D_{k-1}+D_k)}{D_{k-1}} \cdot \dfrac{1}{(u-c_{k-2})(c_{k+1}-u)}$. The limit at c_k from

$\Pi'(u)$ has its minimum, which is

$$\frac{4D_k(1+q_k^-)(1+q_k^+)}{(D_{k-1}+D_k+D_{k+1})^2} = \frac{4(1+q_k^-)(1+q_k^+)}{D_k(1+q_k^-+q_k^+)^2}.$$

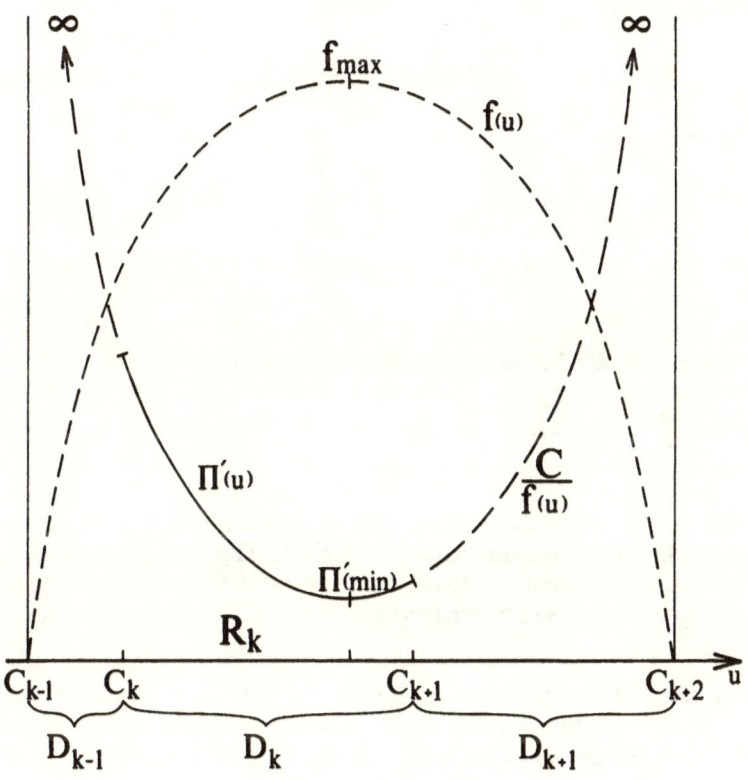

Figure 4. Curve for $\Pi'(u)$ in R_k.

below is obtained by taking here $u = c_k$. The result is the same as in (1).

(3) The limit at c_1 from above is obtained as in (1), with $k = 1$. Hence it is $\dfrac{D_0 + D_1}{D_0 D_1}$.

(4) The limit at c_1 from below is obtained from (14-20)(b) by taking $u = c_1$. The result is the same as under (3).

(5) Similarly, we find that both limits at c_{N-1} are $\dfrac{D_{N-2} + D_{N-1}}{D_{N-2} D_{N-1}}$.

From (14-31):

$$\Pi'(c_{k+1}) = \frac{D_k + D_{k+1}}{D_k D_{k+1}}.$$

Hence

$$\frac{\Pi'(c_k)}{\Pi'(c_{k+1})} = \frac{1 + \dfrac{D_k}{D_{k-1}}}{1 + \dfrac{D_k}{D_{k+1}}}$$

This is $\gtreqless 1$, according as $D_{k-1} \gtreqless D_{k+1}$. Therefore:

(14-32) $\Pi'(c_k) \gtreqless \Pi'(c_{k+1})$ ($k = 1, \ldots, N-1$) according as $D_{k-1} \gtreqless D_{k+1}$.

This means that Π', and hence also $^\bullet\delta$ (14-29), is higher at that end of an interval with the smaller neighbor. This is as it should be, because the probability for the phase point of a new element should be higher where the concentration of old phase points is higher.

(14-33) Let the intervals R_k and R_m ($k, m = 1, \ldots, N-2$) be such that the lengths of R_k and its neighbor intervals are proportional to those of R_m and its neighbor intervals (i.e., $D_{m-1} = CD_{k-1}$, $D_m = CD_k$, $D_{m+1} = CD_{k+1}$, with an arbitrary C), and let u_k in R_k and u_m in R_m be corresponding values (i.e., $u_m - c_m = C(u_k - c_k)$). Then the following holds:

(a) $D_k \Pi'(u_k) = D_m \Pi'(u_m)$.
(b) $D_k {}^\bullet\delta(u_k) = D_m {}^\bullet\delta(u_m)$.
(c) $^\bullet I'(R_k) = {}^\bullet I'(R_m)$.
(d) $c^{**}([R_k], c) = c^{**}([R_m], e)$.

Proof. From the assumptions, $q_k^- = q_m^-$ and $q_k^+ = q_m^+$ (14-14). Therefore

(a) from (14-15)(b), since $u_m - c_{m-1} = C(u_k - c_{k-1})$ and $c_{m+2} - u_m = C(c_{k+2} - u_k)$.

(b) from (a) with (14-29).

(c) from (14-19).

(d) from (c) with (14-28).

We see from (14-33)(a) that, within two intervals with proportional surroundings, $\Pi'(u)$ and therefore $^e\delta$ at corresponding points are inversely proportional to the length of the interval; in other words, it is the more probable for the new element a_N to be represented at this point, the smaller the interval is. This is as it should be. In the classification schema (§2), it was the more probable for a new element to belong to a given cell, the greater the number of old phase points in this cell (see (2-12)); this means, in terms of a quantitative system, the nearer the old phase points in the given region are to each other.

The result (14-33)(d) is important. It says that if two of the interior e-intervals have proportional surroundings, then it is just as probable for the new element a_N to belong to the one as to the other, irrespective of the lengths of the intervals. This result may at first be surprising, but it is easily seen that it is just what should be expected. Suppose that $D_m = 2D_k$. Then, according to (b), the probability density at corresponding points is in R_k twice that in R_m. Therefore, since the length of R_k is one half that of R_m, the probabilities are equal.

The following result concerns the most important special case of (14-33)(c). We shall make use of it in the study of regions with constant interval length (in the next section).

(14-34) Suppose that R_k ($k = 1, \ldots, N-2$) is equal in length to its neighbor intervals, i.e., $D_{k-1} = D_k = D_{k+1}$. Then:

(a) $\Pi'(u)$ for c_k and for c_{k+1} is $\dfrac{2}{D_k}$. (From (14-31)).

(b) Within R_k, $\Pi'(u)$ has its minimum at the midpoint $\frac{1}{2}(c_k + c_{k+1})$; this minimum is $\dfrac{16}{9D_k}$, hence $\frac{8}{9}$ of its value at the end points c_k and c_{k+1}. (From (14-30), since $q_k^- = q_k^+ = 1$.)

(c) $^e I'(R_k) = \frac{8}{3} \ln 2$ ($= 1.84840$). (From (14-19).)

In accordance with (14-33)(a) and (c), the values of Π' in (14-34)(a) and (b) are inversely proportional to D_k, and the value of $^e I'$ in (14-34)(c) is independent of D_k.

15
Regional systems

Summary. A special case of the schema with one magnitude is investigated, in which the intervals R_k between the values given in the evidence are such that they can be divided into several regions, each consisting of intervals of equal lengths. Again theorems for $\prod'(u)$, $\cdot\delta(u)$, and c^{**} are given, some of them of surprising simplicity. They are illustrated by a numerical example ((15-8) and (15-29)) and a curve diagram (fig. 5).

Within the schema with one magnitude, developed in the preceding section, we shall now investigate in greater detail systems of a special kind, which we call *regional systems*. The intervals R_A, $R_1, \ldots, R_{N-2}$, R_B given by the evidence e (14-7) are now assumed to such that (A, B) can be divided into p regions ($p \geq 1$) each consisting of at least three intervals for R_A and R_B. The first and last intervals within a region are called its marginal intervals, the others its interior intervals.

We make the following assumption on D_A and D_B in the regional system. (This will simplify the results, see the remark on (15-9) below.)

(15-1) (a) $D_A = \tfrac{1}{2} D_1$;   hence $D_0 = D_1$.

      (b) $D_B = \tfrac{1}{2} D_{N-2}$;   hence $D_{N-1} = D_{N-2}$.

We shall first determine the course of $\prod'(u)$. (14-34)(a) and (b) yield:

(15-2)   If R_k is any *interior interval* in any region then:

    (a) $\prod'(c_k) = \prod'(c_{k+1}) = \dfrac{2}{D_k}$.

    (b) At the center of R_k, $\prod'$ has its minimum value $\dfrac{16}{9 D_k}$
$$= \tfrac{8}{9} \prod'(c_k)$$

From (14-34)(a) and (15-1)(a): $\prod'(c_1) = \dfrac{2}{D_1}$. This is the minimum of $\prod'$ in R_A, since c_1 is the midpoint of c_0 and c_2 (see the remark following (14-30)). According to (14-20)(b) generally, $\Pi'(A) = \dfrac{D_0 + D_1}{D_A(D_A + D_1)}$; therefore in the present system, with (15-1)(a), it is $\dfrac{8}{3D_1}$. The situation in R_B is analogous.

(15-3) (a) $\Pi'(c_1) = \dfrac{2}{D_1}$.

(b) $\Pi'(A) = \dfrac{8}{3D_1} = \dfrac{4}{3} \Pi'(c_1)$.

(c) $\Pi'(c_{N-1}) = \dfrac{2}{D_{N-2}}$.

(d) $\Pi'(B) = \dfrac{8}{3D_{N-2}} = \dfrac{4}{3} \Pi'(c_{N-1})$.

Now we consider the two *marginal intervals* at the boundary between two regions. Let c_m be the boundary point between two regions. Then R_{m-1} is the last interval of the first region and R_m is the first interval of the second region. Then $D_{m-2} = D_{m-1} \neq D_m = D_{m+1}$. Let us assume that $D_{m-1} < D_m$. We put $q = D_m/D_{m-1}$; then $q > 1$. (As an example, see the relation between the first and the second regions in the later numerical example (15-8) and fig. 5. Here $c_m = c_5$ and $q = 6$. If the first marginal interval is larger than the second, as at c_9 in the example, the results are of course analogous.) We see from (14-32) that $\Pi'(c_{m-1}) > \Pi'(c_m) > \Pi'(c_{m+1})$. More specifically, we find from (15-2)(a), since R_{m-2} and R_{m+1} are interior intervals, the following results:

(15-4) (a) $\Pi'(c_{m+1}) = \Pi'(c_{m+2}) = \dfrac{2}{D_{m+1}} = \dfrac{2}{D_m}$.

(b) $\Pi'(c_{m-2}) = \Pi'(c_{m-1}) = \dfrac{2}{D_{m-2}} = \dfrac{2}{D_{m-1}} = q\Pi'(c_{m+1})$.

From (14-31):

(15-5) $\Pi'(c_m) = \dfrac{D_{m-1} + D_m}{D_{m-1} D_m} = \dfrac{1+q}{D_m} = \dfrac{q+1}{2} \Pi'(c_{m+1})$.

Hence:

(15-6) $\Pi'(c_{m-1}) - \Pi'(c_m) = \Pi'(c_m) - \Pi'(c_{m+1}) = \dfrac{q-1}{2} \Pi'(c_{m+1})$.

Thus at all boundary points between intervals of the second region (c_{m+1}, c_{m+2}, etc.), $\prod'$ has the same value, which is relatively low. At all boundary points within the first region, $\prod'$ has q times that value. At the boundary point c_m between the two regions, the value of $\prod'$ is just the mean of those two values. [If $q > 2$, $\prod'$ decreases throughout R_{m-1}, and also in the greater part of R_m; in R_m it has a minimum at a point near c_{m+1} (the mid point of c_{m-1} and c_{m+2}, (14-30)); this minimum is only a little less than its value at c_{m+1}.] The values of $\prod'$ for the points mentioned are shown in the following table:

(15-7) Table for $\prod'(u)/\prod'(c_{m+g_1})$:

u	generally	for $q = 9$	for $q = 1000$
c_{m-2}	q	9	1000
midpoint	$\frac{8}{9}q$ (min.)	8	888.9
c_{m-1}	q	9	1000
c_m	$\dfrac{q+1}{2}$	5	500.5
c_{m+1}	1	1	1
midpoint	$\frac{8}{9}$ (min.)	$\frac{8}{9}$	$\frac{8}{9}$
c_{m+2}	1	1	1

Thus the overall picture of the curve for $\prod'$, and likewise that for $^*\delta$, in the regional system is as follows. The value of $\prod'$ is the same at all interior boundary points c_k in a region; it is inversely proportional to the length of the intervals of the region. At the midpoint of any two of those points it drops to $\frac{8}{9}$ of the value at the points; this is its minimum in the interval. At the boundary point between two regions the value of $\prod'$ is the arithmetic mean of the values at the interior boundary points in the regions. The value at A is $\frac{4}{3}$ of that at the nearest boundary point; likewise the value at B.

(15-8) *Numerical example.* $N = 14$. Let the values of A, $c_1, \ldots, c_{13}$, B be such that there are three regions with boundaries at c_5 and c_9 (see fig. 5) and with interval lengths $D = 1$, 6, and 2, respectively. Then we find the following values, which are represented by the curve for $\prod'(u)$ in fig. 5. This curve also represents $^*\delta(u)$ (with a different scale), since the latter is proportional to $\prod'(u)$ (14-29); we shall later find: $^*\delta(u) = 0.0396 \prod'(u)$ (15-29).

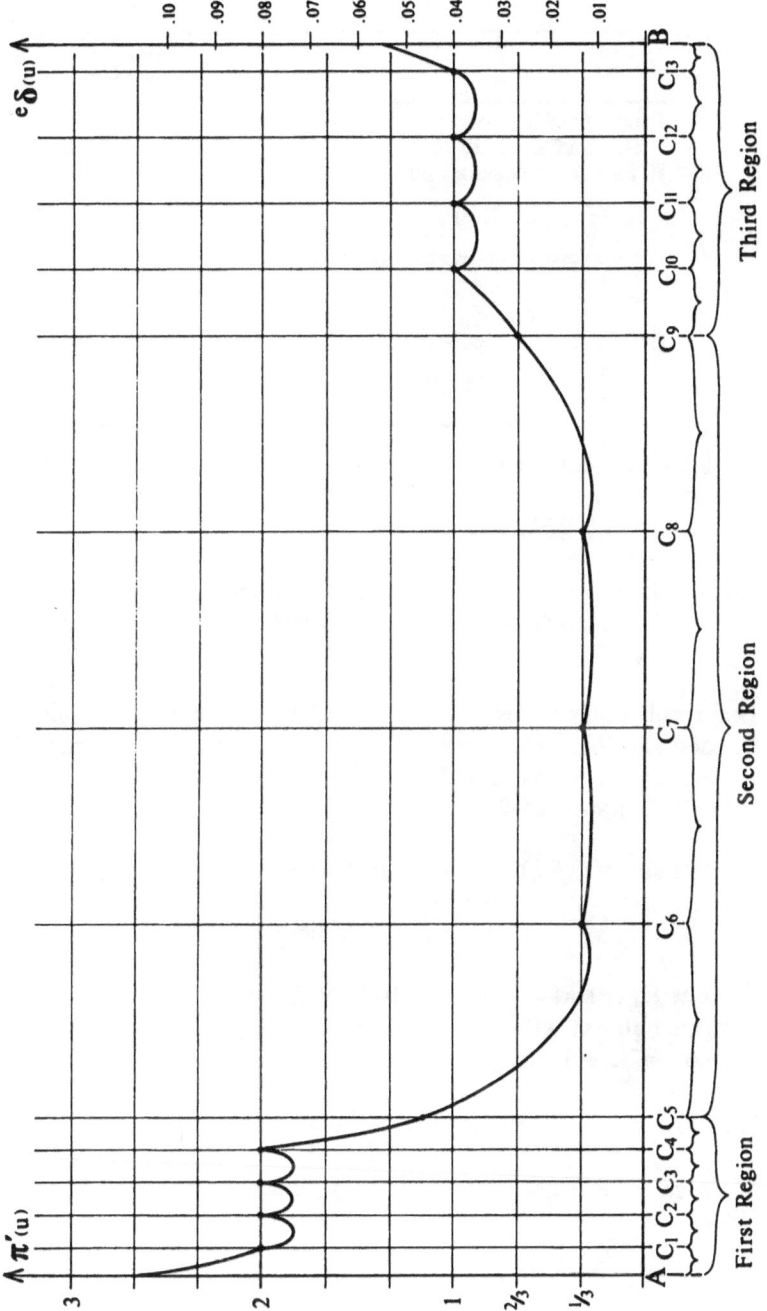

Figure 5. Curve for $\prod'(u)$ and $^e\delta(u)$.

	Regions first	second	third
Length D of intervals (except D_A and D_B) (15-1) D_A and D_B	1 $D_A = \frac{1}{2}$	6	2 $D_B = 1$
Π' for interior boundary points: $\Pi'_b = \frac{2}{D}$ (15-2)(a)	2	$\frac{1}{3}$	1
Π' for midpoints of interior intervals $= \frac{16}{9D} = \frac{8}{9}\Pi'_b$ (15-2)(b)	$\frac{16}{9}$	$\frac{8}{27}$	$\frac{8}{9}$
Π' for the two end points $= \frac{8}{3D} = \frac{4}{3}\Pi'_b$ (15-3)(b)	for A: $\frac{8}{3}$		for B: $\frac{4}{3}$

Now we shall determine the values of 'I' for the intervals in the regional system.

From (14-34)(c):

(14-9) If R_k ($k = 1, \ldots, N-2$) is an interior interval in any region, then 'I'$(R_k) = \frac{8}{3} \ln 2$ ($= 1.84840$). We denote this value by 'C.'

This result holds for $R_2, \ldots, R_{N-3}$ independently of the choice of D_A and D_B. We make the assumption (15-1) in order to assure the validity of (15-9) also for R_1 and R_{N-2}. By the same assumption, with (14-23) and (14-26):

(15-10) (a) 'I'$(R_A) = $ 'I'$(R_B) = \ln 3$ ($= 1.0986$).

(b) $= \frac{3}{8} \cdot \frac{\ln 3}{\ln 2} \cdot C = 0.5944 C$.

Let R_{m-1} and R_m again be two contiguous marginal intervals as described above, with $D_m > D_{m-1}$ and $q = D_m/D_{m-1} > 1$. For R_{m-1}, we have $q^-_{m-1} = 1$ and $q^+_{m-1} = q$. Therefore, with (14-19):

(15-11) $'I'(R_{m-1}) = \frac{2(1+q)}{(2+q)} \ln \left[2\left(1 + \frac{1}{q}\right) \right].$

q may have any value > 1; it is always finite, since $D_{m-1} > 0$ (14-4).

(15-12) (a) $\lim_{q \to 1} {'I'}(R_{m-1}) = \frac{8}{3} \ln 2 = C.$

(b) $\lim_{q \to \infty} {'I'}(R_{m-1}) = 2 \ln 2 = \frac{3}{4} C.$

(a) is obvious, since for $q = 1$ we should have $D_{m-1} = D_m$; thus the two intervals R_{m-1} and R_m would not be marginal but interior. The possible values of $^eI'(R_{m-1})$ are between the above two limits:

(15-13) $$\tfrac{3}{4}C < {^eI'(R_{m-1})} < C.$$

For R_m, we have $q_m^- = \dfrac{1}{q}$ and $q_m^+ = 1$. Hence with (14-19):

(15-14) $$^eI'(R_m) = \frac{2(1+q)}{1+2q} \ln[2(1+q)].$$

(15-15) $$\lim_{q \to 1} {^eI'(R_m)} = \tfrac{8}{3} \ln 2 = C.$$

(15-16) $$^eI'(R_m) > C.$$

As $q \to \infty$, $^eI'(R_m)$ has no finite limit, but it is always finite.

The results are again analogous, of course, if the first marginal interval is larger than the second.

$^eI'(R_e)$ is the sum of the $^eI'$-values of the N intervals in (A, B). Since there are p regions, there are $2p$ marginal intervals and $N - 2p$ interior intervals. Let $c_{m_1}, \ldots, c_{m_{p-1}}$ be the $p-1$ boundary points between the regions. Let $R_{m_j'}$ ($j = 1, \ldots, p-1$) be the smaller and $R_{m_j''}$ the larger of the two marginal intervals adjacent to c_{m_j}. Let $q_j = D_{m_j''}/D_{m_j'}$; hence $q_j > 1$. Then, from (14-27) and (15-9):

(15-17) $$^eI'(R_e) = (N - 2p)C + {^eI'(R_A)} + {^eI'(R_B)} + \sum_{j=1}^{p-1} [{^eI'(R_{m_j'})} + {^eI'(R_{m_j''})}].$$

Now we shall assume that N is large in relation to p. Then only a small fraction of the intervals are marginal. If q_j is small, the $^eI'$-values of the marginal intervals do not deviate very much from C, and hence $^eI'(R_e)$ is near to NC. But with increasing q_j, $^eI'(R_{m_j''})$ grows beyond any bound, as we saw from (15-14). Therefore we shall now examine the situation for large q_j; since we aim only at an approximation for $^eI'(R_e)$, and the number of marginal intervals is small in relation to the total number N of intervals, a rough approximation for the marginal intervals will suffice for our purpose.

(15-18) Approximations for marginal intervals with large q_j (from (15-11) and (15-14)):

(a) $\,^e I'(R_{m_j'}) \cong 2\left(1 - \dfrac{1}{q_j}\right)\left[\ln 2 + \ln\left(1 + \dfrac{1}{q_j}\right)\right].$

(b) $\,^e I'(R_{m_j''}) \cong \left(1 + \dfrac{1}{2q_j}\right)\left[\ln 2 + \ln q_j + \ln\left(1 + \dfrac{1}{q_j}\right)\right].$

(c) $\,^e I'(R_{m_j'}) + {}^e I'(R_{m_j''})$

$\cong 3\left(1 - \dfrac{1}{2q_j}\right)\left[\ln 2 + \ln\left(1 + \dfrac{1}{2q_j}\right)\right]\ln q_j$

$\cong 3\left(1 - \dfrac{1}{2q_j}\right)\ln 2 + \dfrac{3}{q_j} + \left(1 + \dfrac{1}{2q_j}\right)\ln q_j.$

We put:

$$x_j =_{Df} \operatorname{Log} q_j; \quad \text{hence} \quad q_j = 2^{x_j};$$

$$X_j =_{Df} \frac{{}^e I'(R_{m_j'}) + {}^e I'(R_{m_j''})}{C} - 2.$$

Then, from (15-18)(c):

(15-19) Approximations for very large q_j:

(a) $\,^e I'(R_{m_j'}) + {}^e I'(R_{m_j''}) \cong \ln q_j + 3 \ln 2.$
(b) $\qquad\qquad\qquad\qquad \cong (x_j + 3)\ln 2.$
(c) $X_j \cong \tfrac{3}{8}(x_j + 3) - 2 = \tfrac{1}{8}(3x_j - 7).$

(15-20) A few values of X_j as examples (from (15-19)(c)):

x_j	q_j	X_j
10	$2^{10}\ (\cong 10^3)$	2.88
20	$2^{20}\ (\cong 10^6)$	6.63
30	$2^{30}\ (\cong 10^9)$	10.38

From (15-10)(b):

(15-21) $\qquad \dfrac{{}^e I'(R_A) + {}^e I'(R_B)}{C} - 2 = \dfrac{3}{4}\cdot\dfrac{\ln 3}{\ln 2} - 2 = -0.8112.$

Thus we obtain the following approximation for (15-17):

(15-22) $\quad {}^e T'(R_e) \cong C\left[N + \sum_{j=1}^{p-1} X_j - 0.8112\right].$

We see from (15-20) that X_j grows only slowly with q_j. Even for a very large q_j, say 10^9, the corresponding X_j, about 10, may be neglected in (15-22) if N is large, say $>10^4$. Thus:

(15-23) If N is large in relation to p and not many values of q_j are large (say $>10^3$), then ${}^e T'(R_e) \cong NC$.

Thus, under the conditions stated in (15-23), we obtain the following approximate values of the m^{**}-density ${}^e\delta$ with respect to e, and of c^{**} in the regional system.

From (14-29):

(15-24) For any u in (A, B), ${}^e\delta(u) \cong \dfrac{\prod'(u)}{NC}.$

Thus ${}^e\delta(u)$ in the regional system can now be determined with the help of the formulas for $\prod'(u)$ ((14-15), (14-20)(b), (14-24)).

From (14-28):

(15-25) For any interval β within (A, B),

$$c^{**}([\beta], e) \cong \frac{{}^e T'(\beta)}{NC}.$$

The following results are special cases of this. With (15-9):

(15-26) If R_k $(k = 1, \ldots, N-2)$ is an interior interval in any region,

$$c^{**}([R_k], e) \cong \frac{1}{N}.$$

From (15-10)(b):

(15-27) $\quad c^{**}([R_A], e) = c^{**}([R_B], e) \cong \dfrac{3 \ln 3}{8N \ln 2} \cong \dfrac{0.5944}{N}.$

(15-28) Let α be the smaller and β the larger of two contiguous marginal intervals. Let $q = D_\beta/D_\alpha$ ($q > 1$). Then:

(a) $\dfrac{3}{4N} < c^{**}([\alpha], e) < \dfrac{1}{N}$. (From (15-13).)

(b) $c^{**}([\alpha], e) \cong \dfrac{3(q+1)}{4(q+2)N} \cdot \dfrac{\ln\left[2\left(1+\frac{1}{q}\right)\right]}{\ln 2}$,

$\cong \dfrac{3(q+1)}{4(q+2)N}\left[1+\text{Log}\left(1+\dfrac{1}{q}\right)\right]$.
(From (15-11).)

(c) For large q: $\cong \dfrac{3}{4N}\left(1-\dfrac{1}{q}\right)\left[1+\text{Log}\left(1+\dfrac{1}{q}\right)\right]$.
(From (15-8)(a).)

(d) For every large q: $\cong \dfrac{3}{4N}$.

(e) $c^{**}([\beta], e) > \dfrac{1}{N}$. (From (15-16).)

(f) $c^{**}([\beta], e) \cong \dfrac{3(q+1)}{4(2q+1)N}[1+\text{Log}(q+1)]$.
(From (15-14).)

(g) For large q: $\cong \dfrac{3}{8N}\left(1+\dfrac{1}{2q}\right)[1+\text{Log}(q+1)]$.

(h) For very large q: $\cong \dfrac{3}{8N}[1+\text{Log } q]$.

(15-29) *Numerical example.* On the basis of the data in the example (15-8), we obtain the following values of '*I*' with the help of (15-10), (15-11), (15-14), and (15-19).

Interval β	'$I'(\beta)$	$c^{**}([\beta], e)$
R_A	1.099	0.0435
R_B	1.099	0.0435
R_4	1.483	0.0587
R_5	2.842	0.1126
R_8	2.376	0.0941
R_9	1.569	0.0621
sum	10.468	0.4145
Eight interior intervals, each	1.8484	0.0732
together	14.787	0.5856
Sum total	$\Sigma = 25.255$	1.0001

${}^{e}\Gamma$ for R_e, i.e., for the entire interval (A, B), is the sum of the values given for the fourteen intervals; this is $\Sigma = 25.255$. [We see that $NC = 25.878$ is a fair approximation for Σ, in accordance with (15-23); the approximation is not good because $N = 14$ is not large in relation to $p = 3$.] According to (14-28), $c^{**}([\beta], e) = {}^{e}\Gamma(\beta)/\Sigma = 0.0396 \, {}^{e}\Gamma(\beta)$. These values of c^{**} are listed above in the last column. They give the degree of confirmation, on the evidence e, for the hypothesis that $\phi_1(a_N)$ lies in the interval β.

According to (14-29), the density ${}^{e}\delta(u) = \prod'(u)/\Sigma = 0.0396 \prod'(u)$. Therefore the curve in fig. 5 also represents ${}^{e}\delta(u)$. With the values of $\prod'$ from (15-8), we obtain the following values of ${}^{e}\delta$:

Points	$\prod'$	${}^{e}\delta$
Interior boundary points, first region	2	0.080
second region	$\frac{1}{3}$	0.013
third region	1	0.040
A	$\frac{8}{3}$	0.106
B	$\frac{4}{3}$	0.053

www.ingramcontent.com/pod-product-compliance
Lightning Source LLC
Chambersburg PA
CBHW021713230426
43668CB00008B/823